NORTHERN SON

The Boy from the Bush

DICK HUTTON

To: Debra
From — Dick & Kay

PublishAmerica
Baltimore

First printing

Hardcover 978-1-4560-5141-9
Softcover 978-1-4560-5140-2
PUBLISHED BY PUBLISHAMERICA, LLLP
www.publishamerica.com
Baltimore

Printed in the United States of America

I dedicate this story to Kay, my beloved wife of 55 years. Without her support, patience and love, it would have been much different, and certainly not worth writing. She was and is Gods' greatest blessing to me. She is my lover, my confidant, my partner and my friend. We are the nearest thing possible to that "one flesh" spoken of in the Bible.

This is a true story. Some names of people and places have been changed to avoid undue embarrassment of innocents. Some occurrences have been omitted for the same reason and to avoid bruising the sensibilities of the gentle reader. Others, I must admit, have been left out to ease my own conscience. What remains, I hope, is sufficient to draw a clear picture of my life, conversion and hope of Eternal Life in Gods' Kingdom.

Reference: Psalm 23

PART 1

CHAPTER 1

"BEGINNINGS"

I was born on the morning of July 9, 1935 in the comparative luxury of the only hospital in the "Peace River Country" of northern Alberta. The building, on the only high ground in the flooded town-site, was a haven for many that week. Almost every building in town was damaged, and some were swept away—the worst disaster in the towns' short history. It was 2 weeks before my Mother could take me home to the one-room log house on the homestead, 12 miles to the northwest, where I joined my brother, Robert and sisters, Doris and Pearl.

"The farm" was not really a farm. Just a few cleared acres in the bush beside Strong Creek. A cow, an Indian pony, a small chicken house, a two-stall log barn, a big garden and a good well made up the rest of the homestead. The few cultivated acres grew oats for the horse and cow. The chickens fended for themselves, as did the dog and cat.

Beyond our place, to the North, there was nothing but bush, sand ridges, muskeg and more bush. The vegetable garden was central to our survival. Sometimes all we had to eat in the late spring were the produce from the garden that wintered well and wild fruit that my mother had picked and preserved the summer before. We had goose-berries, cranberries, rasp-berries, blue-berries, wild strawberries, black currants and saskatoons in a good year. And, of course, bread—wonderful, mouth-watering bread. Mother baked it twice a week in the oven of her little, wood-burning McLary cook-stove. There is nothing quite like fresh, homemade bread, buttered while it is still hot.

My mother made "the farm" feed us, although she had no electricity, no phone and only her strong hands and willpower to work with. Even the water she used came from a well about 200 feet from the house. She tended the garden, milked the cow and took care of the other animals and all of us kids—alone—for months at a time, summer and winter and managed to be happy most of the time. She sang the old pioneer songs in a strong, near-perfect voice, without any sort of music to accompany her. My father, when he was able, worked for other farmers down on the Roma flats (where the land was better) in the summer as a teamster and farrier. In winter, he cut fire-wood to sell to the ladies in town. But, it seemed that each time the bills were paid, dad would have to spend one or two months in the hospital in Edmonton, 350 miles to the south. Dad was only 5'2" tall and had a speech impediment but other men looked up to him and he was the leader of our little community and the Trustee of our school district.

My father was a physically powerful man, despite his lack of height. He took pride in chopping more wood, hauling more sheaves to the threshing machine and anything else that men could challenge him at. During the times that he was relatively healthy, he worked long hours for small pay. He allowed himself few luxuries other than pipe tobacco and the occasional new shirt or pair of overalls. Although he was sometimes harsh with our mother and us, I think it was the pain and frustration that he suffered all his life that made him that way. Since I was the one who showed the most independence, I was his favourite target. It seemed to me that I would get whacked no matter what I did or why I did it. It took many years, but I was finally able to forgive him before he died. In his strange way, he did love our mother and us and he never drank or otherwise wasted what little money we had. Only once, can I remember my father indulging himself to any great extent. One year, he planted alfalfa along with the regular oat crop and sold the resulting seed for over $800. He bought a matched team of black Perchuron horses, new harness and a new Brantford spring wagon. They were the envy of the entire district, as most of our neighbours were poorer than us.

CHAPTER 2

"ROOTS"

My father was born Joseph Peter Hutton in Paisley, Scotland on June 6, 1898, the son of a wood-craftsman. When he was five years old, his father was killed in a freak accident, plunging the family into poverty, and thus began an unlikely saga. Dads' mother, unable to feed Joseph and his little sister, Hanna, did the only thing she could think of to keep them from starving. She took them to a church orphanage with a promise to come back and get them when she was able to secure well-paying employment. This proved to be more difficult than expected, and when she did return almost 2 years later, she found that Joseph, then 7, had been shipped off to Canada by the well-meaning people of the church. He became one of the famous "Little Immigrants". On arrival in Canada he spent a month at a "Boys' employment depot" before being sent to a farm near Brockville, Ontario as an "Indentured Servant". The terms of his indenture were that he would stay with and work for the McMullen family until he reached the age of 16, at which time he would be paid the sum of 50 English pounds. It was also agreed that he would receive a reasonable Christian education.

While Mr. McMullen exacted his "full money's worth" from my father and treated him harshly, Mrs. McMullen, an English teacher, saw to it that Dad had an exceptional command of the English language. She also taught him arithmetic and other subjects that would serve him well throughout his life. At age 12, he was apprenticed to an "iron monger" and learned to be a blacksmith and farrier (shoeing horses and mules).

When he reached the required age of 16, he stayed on for another few months, and then joined the Canadian Army to fight in the "Great War". After a brief training period and a sea-sick ocean crossing, he found himself in the muddy, blood-soaked trenches of northern France. Three months later, during the battle of Eyeps, his company was almost wiped out by German "Mustard Gas". Then followed long months in an English hospital where the nurses encouraged him to smoke to bring tears to his gas-damaged eyes. He never shook the habit, and smoked a pipe until he died some 60 years later.

Returning to Canada, he went through what was probably the worst time in his life. Although he had sent letters from England and a telegram from Halifax that he was "coming home", he found no one at the train station to meet him. After all these years, he was still not accepted as one of the family. He had visited his mother and sister before coming back to Canada, and for some unfathomable reason, this had an adverse effect on his relationship with Mr. and Mrs. McMullen. They did reconcile many years later, (by mail) but for then, the damage was done. After a short period of time (of which he seldom spoke), he left for the western prairies, never to return. He was just 21 years old.

For the next 8 or 9 years, he worked in Manitoba and Saskatchewan, toiling as a teamster, blacksmith and farrier in the summer and doing odd jobs and record keeping in the city in the winter. He deliberately chose "the hard life", as he put it, just to spite the damage the gas had done to him.

In his 30th year, working as a bell-man, night clerk and handy-man for The Empire Hotel in Regina, he met and married Ethel Cragg. So began the only happy and meaningful chapter of his life.

My mother was born on January 28, 1906 in Saginaw, Michigan to a family of itinerant Canadian workers wintering in the logging camps of the great lakes. Originally from Green Bank, England, they had settled in Ontario and, facing hard times, they had border-hopped to find work. When conditions in Canada improved, they moved north to Gerald, Saskatchewan, about 150 miles east of Regina. Her father, George Cragg, found a good job with the CPR railroad. He operated the station and pump house in Gerald until he retired. As was the custom in those days, he received a gold watch and a railroad pass that allowed him and my grandmother unlimited travel on any railroad in Canada. He was a source of wonder and amazement to me each time he visited our little homestead. He would regale us with stories of the railroad and the places he had been. He entreated my mother to leave her "stone-age hovel in the bush" and return to civilization. But she always demurred and said it was the only place she could be sure of growing enough food to feed her family. There was an under-lying division here that I did not understand until many years later. My mother would have liked a proper lumber-built house and running water, etc. but dad refused to build one in the bush. He would have built one in town, but mom would not move to town.

Getting back to my mother, she grew up in the tiny community and received 3 years of formal education (a lot for a country girl in those days). Where and how she learned to sing remains a mystery to me, but sing he did, to the delight of all who heard. At age 14 she began working out as "the hired girl" on farms and in the homes of "the well-to-do" to help support the growing family of 4 boys and 4 girls. This period of semi-poverty and hard work set the pattern for the rest of her life. People said, "you can always depend on Ethel" and they usually did. My father was no exception. They leaned on each other in good times and bad for the next 25 years.

Working and living in "the Empire" until spring, my father then took a job as a farm manager for that first summer. They both worked hard and got on very well. They lived in a small house on the farm and that plus a good garden helped them prepare for the coming winter. On the 1st day of December the pay ($30 a month) stopped for 3 months but they could remain in the house until April, when the payments would resume. In February, Robert, the first of 8 children was born, and they began to make plans to homestead in "The Peace River Country" of Northern Alberta. When Dad finished seeding the wheat crop, they packed up all their belongings and began the trek of almost 2000 miles to the end of track at Roma, 7 miles west of Peace River town. Dad signed up for a "soldiers' grant" and received a ¼ section of land 6 miles to the north, and, without examining it, he and mom went to work for the contractor who was building the railroad grade west toward Ft. St. John, BC. Mom was the cook and dad was in charge of the horses and mules and spent his days sweating in the blacksmith shop. They worked until freeze-up and then went to build a house on the "grant". What a disappointment! The south half was a swampy stand of black spruce and the rest was a huge sand ridge! Not a good place to start. They walked east and found a quarter on the bank of Strong Creek that was flat and not so heavily forested. There they built their home—a 16' x 18' log cabin with a cedar-shingled roof and a bare board floor. It was a humble dwelling indeed, but my mother kept it whitewashed and scrubbed as if it were a palace until she died some 23 years later.

Both mom and dad worked on the Grand Trunk railway until funds were cut off at the beginning of the "Great Depression". Then began the hardest times they would ever face. Dad worked at whatever he could find, and we lived on "relief" when he was sick. Relief was a form of welfare that was paid back by working for a government road-building crew (at 25 cents an hour) in summer between seeding time and harvest. Mom toiled to meet the never-ending demands of the farm, the children (now 4 with the addition of Doris, Pearl and me), and the livestock—a staunch, stubborn rock of strength and courage in a sea of debt, despair and near-starvation. Through it all, she was able to inject laughter and a sense of pride with her stories of the "good old days" and her songs. Her beautiful voice filled us with awe and happiness in the soft summer evenings and the cold, dark days and nights of the northern winter.

To say that my parents had "true grit" would be the understatement of all time. They were tempered in the fires of adversity and necessity and although they were not church-goers, I am sure that God had a hand in their survival.

CHAPTER 3

"CHILDHOOD MEMORIES"

Memories of my early years, except for the good times, are somewhat clouded and erratic. Not because of age or lack of perception, but because that sometimes cruel and harsh span of years made my memory very selective and protective. I lived in fear of my father, in awe of my mother and in constant friction with my siblings. Not that they were all that bad, rather, it was I who tended toward audacity and rebellion. I felt the sting of moms' willow switch when I did wrong or when I lied. I became, or so I thought, a master of deceit and skullduggery. But I never ceased to love my mother dearly as she patiently guided me through all the lessons of childhood. Wise in so many ways, she was quick to notice my very early changes toward manhood. When I was about 8 years old, she sat me down and explained sex to me in a way that I'll never forget. I grew up knowing that it wasn't "dirty", but was to be respected and very private. She answered my few questions about girls and told me that if I ever had a problem to come to her and we would work it out. My father was another matter. He used his work-hardened hands to rain retribution on the head of his "recalcitrant boy", upon my mother and even upon the animals of our little homestead. The summer I turned 12, I finally said "enough!" I looked at my father in the eye, (I was 6 inches taller than he was), and, without raising my voice, I told him that if he ever struck me or mom again I would find a way, fair or fowl, to make him pay for it. He thought about that for a minute, then turned away. I never had to make good on my threat.

But life wasn't all bad, and I remember the good times with amazing clarity. Playing in "the deep place" of Strong Creek, or in the dust, mud or snow (it seemed to make little difference) with my younger brother, Tom and our dog, Bud. There was a Taffy-pull each time our Uncle Victor, Aunt Margaret and cousins Lucy and Ruth visited. We rode our horse, Peggy (more about her later) when we could catch her and went on adventures up the St. Germaine trail, which followed the creek north to a marshy muskeg lake. Another lake to the west yielded wild hay and haying time was exciting in spite of the work and sweat involved. Bill Dundas, our nearest neighbour and Dad would pool resources each summer, sharing equipment, labour and whatever else they had. Then there was threshing time when all the farmers took their horses, wagons, bundle-racks and Bill Evans' McCormack Deering separator from farm to farm until everyone had their harvest in. Our little field of oats was threshed out in about an hour, but the crew always managed to be at our house for supper. My mother's skill at the cook-stove being legendary. Our parents were all too busy to keep track of us as we ran rampant through the house, barn and granary. Amazingly, none of us were ever seriously hurt as we ran around the horses and machinery. The fall after my 12th birthday I finally got my wish to participate in the harvest.

I and a 15 year old friend, Stanley Wilson, were entrusted with my dads' precious team of blacks. We worked our hearts out to keep up with the others. After the first day, we were so tired we could hardly eat supper, but we were up the next morning to go at it again. After a couple of days of teasing and cat-calling the other men finally accepted us, and we became part of the crew. My mother told me how proud she was of me and that meant more to me than anything else.

Sometimes I sit and recall fragments of things that happened as if they were part of a disjointed dream. Running into a barbed wire fence at dusk, cutting myself above the eye. Riding horses in a late night thunderstorm. Pushing myself for miles on my first sled. Xmas get togethers. Injuring my hand in an old, discarded set of gears, causing my mother to take me, late at night, to the hospital for repairs. Long winter nights playing "500" or working on jigsaw puzzles. Being stung 50-100 times by hornets stirred up by Peggy in one of our many skirmishes to get her into the barn or corral or whatever.

Let me tell you about Peggy. In the winter of 1928-29, just before "The Depression" began, my folks had purchased all the worldly goods of an Englishman who had given up on the frontier and was going back to the "old country". They included a Mclary cook-stove, a fancy wooden cupboard, matching table & chairs, a 4-wheeled, one horse shae and an 1,100 lb. Indian pony named "Peggy". The person who named her Pegasus (from Greek mythology) was either deluded or playing a cruel joke on her future owners. Although she was always there when we needed her most, she was at times possessed of the devil himself. She took great pleasure in dumping people (adults and kids alike), breaking harness or buggy by backing into the bush or running away. You had to love her or despise her, depending on the moment. She pulled the whole family to school, to town, to picnics and home again many hundreds of times. She was solely responsible for the third (middle) rut in the St. Germaine Trail, from the great muskeg along Strong Creek to the Peace River. She was known far and near. Cursed by some, admired by others. I remember some of her destructive binges, but I also remember how still and quiet she stood when a buggy wheel got caught in the track of the railroad bridge and had to be lifted out carefully to prevent the precious wheel from being twisted and smashed beyond repair. She seemed to sense that there was a time for play and destruction and a time for serious work when any of us were in danger, sick or just worn out. I have been spared the knowledge of how Peggy died, but I know she was near 25 years old. I also know, in my heart, that she didn't die before she was ready. Peggy never did anything before she was ready. If there are horses in God's Kingdom, I'm sure I will get to scratch and pet old Peggy again—that is, if I can catch her.

I remember our wooden, battery-operated radio. It didn't have the little batteries of today, but instead, large clumsy "power-packs". Bigger and heavier than the radio itself. A 50' antennae, strung between 2 tall poles on insulators, with a connecting wire running down the side of the house through a "lightening arrester" and an iron grounding rod completed the setup. The power packs were good for about 200 hours and that time was not wasted. We listened to selected weekly shows, the news and, of course, "Hockey Night in Canada" with Foster Hewitt and the Toronto Maple Leafs. I suspect that my mother listened to the first real soap operas in the morning when we were away at school. She seemed to be right up to date when she visited with friends.

I recall much of life on the homestead by lamplight. Dim coal oil lamps at first, with their wicks and glass chimneys. Then our first real taste of luxury—a pressurized kerosene lamp that produced at least 300 watts of light and quite a bit of heat in our little whitewashed house. It made many trips to our school for meetings, Xmas concerts and the like. It had to be kept burning during these trips to protect the ash mantles. My wife still owns one of these relics of the frontier. It's fitted with bulbs and a plug-in cord now. Most people today can't imagine life without electricity and I hope we never have to go back to those dark days. We would survive but only the most imaginative would call it "living". But, enough of trivia, let us get on with the part of my early life I enjoyed the most—school!

CHAPTER 4

"SCHOOL DAYS"

Peace View School. There was no view of the Peace River or anything else much either. Four acres carved out of the boreal forest, one corner of which was occupied by a 20' x 40' schoolhouse, a teacherage, a playground, 2 outhouses and a huge woodpile. There was no power or telephone. There was not even a barn, as most of the rural schools had in those days. It was as sorry a place to educate children as could be found, but to me it was a grand cathedral. It was a place where my hungry brain could soak up knowledge. It was also a place where I stood out from others because of my craving for more and more information about the wonderful world outside our corner of the "great depression" and WW II. Beyond the dirt roads, the poverty and the hopelessness of "Improvement District #44", as our backward little patch of northern Alberta was known. I somehow knew, as early as age 6 that I must arm myself for the future, if I were to have a future. I knew that I must absorb all the knowledge and know-how that was available to me. With the help and guidance of our beloved (and terrifying) teacher, Mrs. Bud Kent, I managed to take 2 grades in one year—3 times! At age 12, I finished grade 9 by correspondence under her tutelage and took my exams at the high school in town with honours!

I'll never forget Mrs. Kent; I loved her and feared her at the same time. When I finished my work before others, it was not time to sit on my hands—oh no, she immediately found something harder and more advanced for me to do. And woe betide me if I slacked off! Imagine a shy, introverted 11-year-old boy in a school with 20 girls! That's how I spent grade 8! No wonder I learned so fast; there was nothing else to do. A boy can't get into much trouble when there are no other boys to scheme with. Mrs. Kent kept a sharp eye on the girls so that playtime wasn't too awful for me. Mrs. Kent was a woman of many talents. Her first task with a new student was usually to teach them to understand and speak English, then on the reading and writing. It must have been frustrating teaching the first 2 grades. There were Russians, Germans, Hungarians, Poles and one Swedish family. She must, at times, have lived on sheer will power and aspirin. But to the good fortune of myself and many others, she never gave up. Even on the weekends she had to put up with a ne'r-do-well, alcoholic husband. In addition to our schoolwork, she taught us to sing, act, sew and cook (me too). She was also our self-appointed health administrator. She always had us ready for our Xmas concert with plays, choral recitations and songs. Then for the music festival in the spring, where we added public speaking to our repertoire. She must have taught us pretty well, as we brought home the overall award more often than not. "The Cup" would then grace our humble school in an honoured place beside the main blackboard for 10 months or so until it was time to try to win it again. As if that were not enough, she then trained us for the big summer sports meet in Grimshaw! One year I will never forget. Mrs. Kent got everyone together and they made uniforms for the sports meet. The material was flour and sugar sacks, bleached white and some dyed blue, to outfit each of us in blue shorts and white tops with the words "PEACE VIEW" across the back! What a sight we were when we appeared on the sports field! I can still hear the hoots and catcalls of the town kids! But we won, and won, and won and went home happy, in spite of our sunburned arms and legs. Yes, she some kind of school-marm. I know now that she was a blessing sent straight from Heaven to us all.

CHAPTER 5

"THE WAR YEARS"

I remember when the Second World War started, even though I was only 4 years old. I especially remember "PEARL HARBOR". We heard it first on the 6 o'clock news. Our nieces, Lucy and Ruth were there and through the static of our old radio it seemed they were talking about Coal Harbour, where their father was working for the winter. A lot of tears were shed before the matter was cleared up. The war caused drastic changes in all our lives. First, all the young men volunteered or were "called up". Then dad tried to enlist, much to my mother's chagrin. However, his attempt turned out to be a small blessing in disguise for us. It was only then that the full extent of WW 1 injuries came to light, and he was able to extract a small pension from the government. My father spent the war alternately cursing Hitler then "The Jews" for causing it.

Then came rationing! Rationing of almost everything. Butter, sugar, tea, coffee liquor, anti-freeze and tires. As we had no use for the latter 3, we were able to trade our ration stamps for plenty of the former. Others were not so fortunate.

Uncle Vic, who had 1 or only 2 cars in the district, patched and re-patched inner-tubes and used old tires and binder canvas as "boots" inside the tire casings. The rations of alcohol-anti-freeze soon evaporated and the engine had to be drained when not in use. A large kettle of water was kept hot on the cook-stove in case the car had to be used unexpectedly. Many non-rationed things were hard to get and most mail orders from Simpson's or Eaton's came back with substitutes or "out of stock" slips.

The war with Japan brought a lot of excitement to our neck of the woods. The Alaska Highway was built in 1943-1944 to carry goods and military equipment to Alaska to protect against Japanese invasion. Until a new bridge could be built across the Peace River at Taylor, B.C., everything had to be trucked across our combination train and traffic bridge. Also a refinery had to be built at Norman Wells, NWT to supply (via pipeline to white Horse, Yukon) diesel fuel to the highway builders. All this had to be sent in by way of the Mackenzie highway from Grimshaw AB north to Hay River NWT, then by barge to Norman Wells. The US army built a huge camp and stationed 1000 soldiers across the river from town to strengthen and protect the bridge. We all understood that there was a danger of sabotage, but the anti-aircraft gun emplacements were a standing joke. There wasn't an aircraft in the world that could fly that far, let alone get back. The Americans seemed to enter all parts of our lives. They cut and hauled cordwood for their camps night and day. They flocked to all the social events for miles around. Some of the young women, including my cousin Ruth, married soldiers, while others just bore their children. There wasn't anything anyone could do abut the situation, with over 1000 lonely soldiers in an area that had been drained of its young men to fight in Europe. When the war was over, they simply left, leaving behind a mountain of supplies, machinery, ordinance, and of course, many broken hearts.

The war was boon to us in many ways. Businessmen grew fat on soldier's pay. For the first time in 15 years there were jobs for all who could work. Even our lowly bush rabbits were in demand. Their fur was used to line airmen's flying suits. 10 cents a skin! Not much by today's standards, but dad could snare and shoot 50 in a good day. $100-$150 a month, about twice what a man could earn at a good job. The war was also an education for us, and I began to dream of places I would go to see when I grew up. The stories the men told and the news on the radio served to make me terribly discontented with life in the backwoods. The war ended just one month after my tenth birthday.

CHAPTER 6

"GROWING UP FAST"

The next 3 years wrought a drastic change in my life. I grew with leaps and bounds, both physically and mentally. At age 10, I could harness and hitch a team of horses by myself, haul straw in winter and help build fences in summer. Now that dad had his prized team of Perchurons, there was a lot more work to do. I hauled firewood to sell. I hauled timbers for a new barn, ploughed my mother's garden, and many other chores. I even helped shingle the new barn. Peggy was sort of pensioned off but still useful on occasion.

At this point, I must tell you about my sister, Pearl. Four years older than I, she excelled at school and helped mom and dad more than any of the family. Among other things, she designed and helped build our new barn with its shingled, hipped roof and timbered floor. It was a far cry from any other building on the farm, including our house. She had much more staying power than any of the rest of us. She "hung in there" through good times and bad. She was the only one of us who finished high school and went on to a life-long profession—teaching—

in the steps of our dear Mrs. Kent. She was the "anchor" of the family. When we had all dispersed to our various paths in life, Pearl stayed with dad and Tom. She put herself through "normal school" for teachers, helped tom through high school and helped dad through his declining years. From age 17 she became the centre of the family. Although the rest of us didn't keep in touch with each other, we always touched base with Pearl occasionally for the rest of our lives. My relationship with her was to become the purest form of brother-sister love that God intended.

My older brother and sister, Bob and Doris, left home of necessity before finishing elementary school, so I hardly knew them until much later in life. Tom, my youngest brother, was born to be a trucker and among other substantial accomplishments, came to own his own transport company.

As mentioned previously, I excelled in school. The summer I finished grade 9, Peace View School was closed and Mrs. Kent was retired. The schoolhouse was soon mysteriously destroyed by fire. Gossip had it that Mrs. Kent had set the fire, and I'm sure that no one would have blamed her. Now, all the students in the district would be bussed to Peace River, where I entered grade 10 at age 13. This time, to me, was the beginning of a great disillusionment. I had handled a bundle team for the last 2 seasons and proudly kept up with the men in all respects. I felt I had become a man, and took it very seriously. Now, I was back in school with "children"—all 4 years older than I, but children all the same. I didn't like them and the feeling was mutual. Even the teachers seemed to resent the whiz-kid from the bush. No more going to head of the class, no more special attention—only trouble—and I could see no end to it.

Then my mother, who had been sick with cancer for over a year, was hospitalized for what we knew was the final time. She died at xmas time. My last image of her was sitting up in a hospital bed with the family all around her, tears streaming down her cheeks. At that moment my heart broke and I remember very little of the next 4 months. A hazy recollection of being in a church (for the first time) at her funeral, driving the team and sleigh to the cemetery and little else. I recall nothing of going back to the farm with Pearl and tom, or going to town later to live with cousin Ruth and her American soldier husband. My next recollections are of April and the beginning of spring

It was also the beginning of my resolve to leave. I didn't think about it as running away—just leaving the whole mess behind and starting a new life. Ruth and Elmer had tried to make a new home for me and I loved them for it, but it was time to go. There were no thoughts of failure or return—I wasn't coming back. My plans made, I took 2 blankets, some food, and leaving no word with anyone, I caught the bus for Grimshaw. I remember that short trip well. I wasn't afraid: I was just angry at the whole world and determined to make it on my own.

CHAPTER 7

"TRANSITION"

I arrived at the Grimshaw Hotel with $1.75 in my pocket. My first purchase was a package of Daily Mail tobacco, a book of Vogue cigarette papers and a small box of matches. This completed my image of what a man out to be. Total cost—$0.47. I bought a cup of coffee for a nickel and sat at a table by the front window where I could watch the trucks coming in off the Mackenzie Highway with their loads of wheat, fish and lumber. Lumber—that was the key to my plans. I knew the lumber companies to the north were always short of help and would hire almost anyone, as long as they could work. I was sure that my size, strength and knowledge of horses would net me a job of some sort in a lumber camp. As I smoked my first cigarette, I watched the first load of lumber being dumped in the big yard across the street. As I was getting up to go flag it down, it came right across the street and parked in front of the hotel. The driver and two women got out and came in for coffee. I screwed up my courage and went over to their table to give the driver my much-rehearsed speech. I needed a job and did he know where I might find one? He looked me up and down, and with a friendly grin, asked if I had ever worked in a sawmill. I said no but I would give it my best shot. He and the women (the cook and her helper), began poking fun at me and assuring me there was indeed work for me at Fisher's Mill but since there were 3 in the cab already, I would have to ride on the back or wait until he came back the next day. I said I would ride on the lumber deck and it was settled. If I didn't freeze to death on the 165-mile trip, I had a job.

From that point on, everything was new and I resolved to meet each obstacle as it came and not worry in the meantime. We arrived at the mill in time for supper. Everyone seemed happy and content so I just went with the flow and kept my eyes and ears open. I had heard it said, "you don't learn anything with your mouth open", so I kept mine shut. That little bit of wisdom would serve me well I the months and years to come. I bedded down that first night on a straw tick on the floor of a huge bunkhouse, happier than I had been for a long time.

The next morning, my good fortune deserted me. The mechanical slab conveyor, which took the waste from the head-saw to the fire pit had broken down. The foreman said I was just the lad to fill in until it was fixed. Lugging the 40lb. green slabs 20 feet to the fire pit wasn't too bad at first but by dinnertime I was exhausted. I ate my meal and stretched out for a rest. It seemed like only a few minutes and the whistle was summoning us back to work. The afternoon went by in a blur of aching arms and legs, but somehow I made it to quitting time. Supper, of course, was out of the question. I stumbled to my newly constructed bunk and collapsed—winter clothes, boots and all. At about 7 o'clock the "bull cook", (as camp attendants were called in those days), brought me a plate of food and a cup of coffee. After I'd eaten he suggested I walk around for a bit or I'd be stiff as a board in the morning. Good advice—I was already stiff as a board, I hurt with every move, but the pain eased a little after I walked down to the horse barns and back. I have never slept more soundly than I did that night.

The next day the slab conveyor had been repaired and I was sent to work on the "green chain", sorting and piling the fresh-cut lumber as it came from the mill. This was supposed to be the hardest, most hated job in the mill, but after my ordeal by fire (literally) the day before, it was a piece of cake. I even got to roll and smoke a couple of cigarettes. The crew accepted me as a young man; my claim to being 17 years old was never disputed. After a few days I began to feel comfortable with my new life.

The Mounties were coming!!! The bull cook brought me the word. He'd seem them start up the mill road two miles away. I had to move fast. I rolled up everything I had accumulated in my blankets and took off through the bush. I walked straight east until I came to the Mackenzie highway about 10 miles away. I then hitched a ride to Knotekiwan, the nearest village. To this day, I don't know if the police were looking for me or not, but I'd had a taste of freedom and earning my own way and I wasn't about to let them ruin everything. I hid out for a couple of days, then visited my sister Doris who was living on a farm in the area with her husband and the first 2 of 8 children. When I felt the hue and cry, (real or imagined) had died down, I went to the new town of Manning to find the second of the dozens of jobs I would have over the next 20 years.

I found work at a service station, but was let go after a week. Then I worked in a butcher shop while I waited to go back to the lumber camps where I would be much safer. One day I saw a lumber truck with an old man at the wheel and, on impulse, flagged him down and repeated my well-worn request for a job, particularly with horses. In half an hour I was headed for Paddle River with Bill Williamson, owner of Williamson Sawmills. I soon realized I had scraped the bottom of the lumber business. The truck was old and cranky and the last few miles of mud road were almost impassable. The camp wasn't much better. The log kitchen and commissary were in good shape, but the owner's quarters, bunkhouse and barn were in sorry condition. The mill itself was an old steam outfit converted to diesel power and the big Sawyer-Massey steam tractor still stood in position, supposedly ready to take over if the diesel failed. I met the crew—one Indian (little Henry) about 30 years old and a big half-breed (Big Henry) about 20, with a mean disposition. Bill's son, Jack was the sawyer and his wife helped his mother with the cooking and chores. Again, I bedded down on a straw tick on a wooden bunk. Supper was plain but good and I began to relax.

Then Old Bill took me down to see the horses. I saw at once this was the heart of the operation. The 4 big bays in the corral were the most welcome sight I had seen since leaving home. I ran my hands over them as Bill questioned me closely about my ability as a teamster. Apparently satisfied, he told me I would be taking over the skidding in the morning with the 2 mares. I was ecstatic, so much so that I didn't notice the anger on the big half-breed's face as we turned in.

The next day was a blur of activity. The two mares responded to my experienced, gentle hand and worked willingly until noon. I unharnessed them, rubbed them down and fed them before going for my own dinner. When we finished, I had my first run-in with Big Henry. I had taken his favourite job and he didn't like it. Fearfully, I stood my ground but I knew this wasn't over. I worried about him all afternoon as I worked the other two horses as successfully as I had the two mares in the morning. The day flew by. I finished tired but satisfied. I knew from Old Bill's grin that I had put in a good day's work.

After supper I went down to the barn and spent some time with the horses. Little Henry came by and told me not to worry about big Henry. Then I was really scared, or perhaps I should say terrified. I had never had a serious fight with anyone and I felt I was going to take my first licking. I walked back to the bunkhouse, and sure enough, Big Henry was waiting for me on the doorstep. He stood up and told me I was about to learn a lesson. I was afraid to back down, knowing it would be impossible to stay if I did, so I took the best stance I could on my shaking legs. Big Henry took a couple of steps toward me, then stopped. To my surprise, he dropped his hands and saying something about not being able to beat up on a little kid, turned and went inside. Then I heard Little Henry chuckle behind me. I turned, and there he stood, axe handle in hand and a look of great satisfaction on his face. He hadn't said a word, but Big Henry had gotten the message loud and clear. As spring gave way to summer, we finally became friends, in a way that only men sharing hard work can.

I became expert at skidding logs out of the hills to the mill. All went well until one hot day, just after a heavy rain, when I was bringing down the big butt logs that we saved for the wet, slippery days, the mares suddenly stopped. I knew that one was in foal but I had no idea she was so close to her time.

I looked on in terror as she lay down in the mud to give birth to her colt. I froze for a moment and then began furiously to unbuckle her harness and collar and pull it away from her muddy, staining body. I thought she was going to die, and the colt too! Then help arrived—the whole crew—including Old Bill. When the panic was over, everyone had a good laugh at my first attempt at midwifery. I was finally able to laugh with them.

The mill shut down for 2 months in the summer, so I drew my pay and went to town with the rest. I took a room at the only rooming house in town and soon had a job with Robertson Construction. For the first few days I picked roots and brush off a newly graded bush road. Hard work for small pay, but a 14-year-old boy has got to eat. I was befriended by one of the machine operators, Dave Garnet, and was soon operating the grader that he pulled with his TD-14 crawler tractor. After a few days, he taught me how to operate the "cat" as well. He also taught me to drink and I took my first fateful steps toward alcoholism. A few beers, and I became the life of the party, singing all the popular songs and the many old songs my mother had sung. I had a natural tenor voice and an almost photographic memory for lyrics, which went well with Dave's enthusiastic efforts on his Gene Autry guitar. I learned a lot of wrong things that summer, but I relished every minute. Finally, the good times began to end in arguments and fights. Alcohol gave me courage that I did not come by naturally and after many a bloody nose and black eye, I decided to leave the outfit for something less dangerous.

Going from one extreme to the other, I found a job on a farm near North Star, Alberta just in time for harvest. The farmer's name was Frederickson. He grew clover and milked 8 cows, selling the milk door to door in Manning and North Star each day. I liked driving the tractor in the field but I hated the dairy barn. The milking and bottling wasn't bad, but the barn had to be cleaned twice a day and I did not like that. The tedium of the farm was broken each weekend when I rode my bike to town and took in whatever entertainment was available. Then, on Sunday, broke and hung-over, I would peddle my way back to the farm. It was on one such trip that I met my first girl. I had known many girls in the past and had even liked some of them, but this was a woman! Blonde, blue-eyed, at least 16 or 17 years old and on top of that, she really seemed to like me. I was smitten! We talked for a little while, or rather she talked and I tried to follow, then she asked me over to her Grandmother's house the next day after work. I went home in a daze. Nobody had prepared me for this!

CHAPTER 8

"THE MAKING OF A MAN"

I stayed at the farm until late November, mainly because of my attraction to Thelma Simpson. She was still in school and had been raised by her Grandmother since birth. We went to the movies on the weekends and spent many hours in Granny's living room, just talking and listening to the radio. We sang all the popular songs and played cards with Granny and Thelma's uncle, Norman. Granny treated me just like one of her many sons and when I got a winter job in the "oil patch", I stayed at their house on my days off. I had no vehicle so I had to hitchhike or ride my bike everywhere I went, thus I was no stranger to frostbite. I once walked from North Star to the Simpson store (8 miles) in the middle of the night at -40 degrees F. I liked my job as a "jug-hustler" and was soon helping the "shooter" load the shot-holes with high explosives. I loved the hurry-hurry of the daily quest for more and more "production".

The first week in January, a strange thing happened to me. The crew I worked with went on strike for higher pay. This was the best job I had ever had and I felt no loyalty to the others, so I remained on the job. A new crew was hired, but since I was the only one with experience loading the shot-holes, I was given a crash course in "shooting". I worked hard and when the old crew came back (for the same pay as before), I kept the job. The fact that I had no explosives license and was too young to write for one meant little in that place and time. I was kept on even after the prospect was finished and we headed south to Grimshaw to beat the road-ban in April. Along the way, the party chief promised to take me to Texas and make a "real" shooter out of me. I was so excited I forgot about my age and when the time came to produce a birth certificate or driver's license as ID, I was devastated. My dreams of the Texas oilfields were smashed! I went to my room and cried for the first time since my mother had died. The next day, frustrated and disappointed, I drew my pay and caught a bus to Dawson Creek, BC. From there I traveled up the Alaska Highway to White Horse, Yukon territory looking for work. Finding none, and running low on money, I returned to Dawson Creek and there began one of the most exciting adventures of my life.

I was sitting in the coffee shop of the Dawson Hotel with $17.50 in my pocket wondering how I would make it through the weekend when I was approached by a soldier. Now I had met many military men in my short life, but this guy was different. In spite of the sharp uniform, shiny shoes and Staff Sergeant's Insignia, he was casual and friendly, even boisterous as he offered to buy me a hot meal "on the army". He knew his job well, and before I realized it, I had signed up to take the recruiting exam at #10 Manning Depot, Calgary. I thought, what the heck, I might as well get a few meals and a warm place to sleep until they asked for proof of my age. They never did! Over the next two weeks, I had my first ride on a train, my first look at a Canadian army base, and the dubious honour of finishing in the top 10 of 200 raw recruits in the entrance exams. I didn't realize it then, but not one of the 200 was rejected. The casualty lists from Korea were getting longer and longer and most of them—kids, bums, Indians and Métis—wound up in the same place, the 2nd Division, Princess Patricia's Canadian light Infantry. After a very short training period they were shipped, via Fort Lewis, Washington to the faltering U.N. front line facing the Chinese Communists. I, on the other hand, was given a choice and I chose the Armoured Corps. I thought I'd be safer in a tank. Was God guiding me even then?

We were very shortly shipped out to Camp Borden, Ontario. #12 Manning Depot, Royal Canadian Armoured Corps Training School. The trip was a lark. New country, new faces, new smells and even new booze. I don't know where all the liquor came from, but the boys liked to hear me sing, so it flowed freely for three days and nights. Rye, scotch and rum were the most popular, but we sampled almost everything else including some sweet, milky liqueur that an Arab had in little 4oz jars. One spoonful per drink was plenty. I gained the name "One Drink" because of my propensity for bursting into song after only one or two strong drinks in the morning. The trip must have been awful for the ordinary travelers on the train, but in those days, Canadian men going off to war were still held in very high regard by the public and authorities alike, so no one got into serious trouble.

The third and last day of the trip was different. We were all herded into two day-coaches and shunted off on to a spur line that ran right into camp some 50 miles from Barrie, Ontario. A steady downpour followed us all the way and the remaining booze was confiscated, so we arrived in a very sombre and weary manner. We walked, soaking wet, for about 2 miles in the dark and rain and were herded into a gloomy "H" hut with nothing but seemingly endless rows of bunks, bare bulbs in the ceiling, and the hiss of steam from the antique heating and shower facilities in the center. We all agreed that the party was indeed over.

I awoke with a headache and immediately forgot about it in the din around me. A 5'-6" demon with a moustache and Corporal's chevrons on his sleeves was striding up and down the floor shouting commands faster than I could decipher them, but I got the message. I was in the army and it was time—0530 hrs—to get up and start the day—at the double. In the space of 20 minutes we were washed, shaved, dressed and "on parade" in front of the H-hut. There, we were told that we were the sorriest looking bunch of bums he had ever seen and sent to line up for breakfast. We were apprised of the fact that while we could eat as much as we wanted, we only had 15 minutes to do it. Then, led by our cocky Corporal Heath, we marched as best we could to the mysterious Quarter Master's Stores, where we drew our "kit" and said farewell to our "civvies".

We were deloused, showered, dressed, had our hair cut and were led back to our barracks to begin washing, shining and polishing our new possessions, a process that never ended. At 1200hrs we were "on parade" again. None of us had done anything right as far as Corporal Heath and our new Sergeant Jessup were concerned. They despaired loudly and at great length of ever turning us into soldiers. I must admit we were a sorry sight. We had dinner, and then were introduced to close-order drill on the parade square. What a disaster!!! I'm sure they did it just to show us how clumsy and uncoordinated we were. When we finally stopped at 1700hrs, we were exhausted, despairing and most of all, angry. I'm sure I was not the only one to think of taking off that first night, but as it turned out we didn't have time. Our little Corporal spent 4 hrs showing us how to properly clean, polish, press and shine our "kits". Sometimes teaching, sometimes criticizing, sometimes cursing, but always shouting. There was never any question about what he said; I'm sure the guys two huts over heard every word.

Next morning, after a somewhat less rigorous inspection and breakfast, we were told that the normal 16-week course had been shortened to 8 weeks and they just might be able to pound enough sense into us to see us through and keep us from getting killed. They would now entrust us with rifles. No ammunition, just the rifles. These rifles would be our constant companions, day and night, from then on. I could hardly wait to demonstrate my shooting skills with my much used and much polished 303 British Enfield. Later on we were given ammunition and taught to shoot, army style, and I did quite well. We all knew that, in Korea, we would be issued US and UN standard weapons, but for now we had to make do with WW2 left-overs. Browning 303 Bren-guns, 9MM sten-guns and pistols, electrically fired anti-tank weapons, #36 shrapnel grenades, ancient Churchill tanks (which no longer worked but had to be kept shiny and clean anyway) and other out-dated museum pieces. With these and constant instruction, close order drill, obstacle courses and route marches of 5, 10 and 15 miles long, we prepared for war!

After the first 4 weeks, which went by in a blur of shouting, exhaustion, heat, dust and sore, aching muscles, we were given a 24 hr. pass to Toronto. Danny (Trooper Douglas D. MacDonald, SF21880) and I who had become fast friends after having a fight, promptly overstepped the limits of our pass and went to Buffalo, New York. Homing in like radar on the red light district, we got drunk, got robbed and got kicked out of our room in short order. We hitchhiked back and reached camp 4 hrs late. We were then faced with the wrath of our 2 NCOs and the rest of the troop, who had been confined to quarters for a week because of our misdeeds. We received much abuse from our fellow troopers over the next week while Corporal Heath turned a blind eye.

Somehow, we got through the final 4 weeks of Basic Training. The day we finished, Corporal Heath, Sergeant Jessup, Lieutenant St. Laurent and the Regimental Sergeant major responsible for our training pronounced us one of the best units that had ever passed through their hands. They issued dire warnings of what lay ahead in advanced training with our chosen regiments and "across the pond" in Korea. They also issued a 48 hr. pass to each of us.

This, we decided, was our last chance at freedom. Danny was lonesome for his girl in Halifax and it didn't take much talking for me to agree to go AWOL with him. We hit Toronto Friday night and didn't even slow down. Hitchhiking was easy in our uniforms but after our passes ran out we had to trade in our kit for some civvies with the last of our money. By strange coincidence, we changed clothes in Brockville, Ontario where my father had grown up. It was a good thing we kept our army-issue boots, because a bylaw forbidding hitchhiking forced us to walk the full length of Montreal Island, some 26 miles.

This trip was an adventure in itself. Illegally out of uniform, AWOL, broke and hungry, we hitchhiked night and day. We watched the Thousand Islands appear out of the morning mist, watched workers cutting peat on the Gaspe Peninsula, and drove a truck while its driver slept for 200 miles. One morning, we woke up in hay filled barn almost immobile with cold. The hay served as a covering for a huge pile of sawdust, which in turn covered about 80 tons of ICE!!! It had been cut the previous winter for use in the dairy industry. I still shiver when I think of it. We worked 3 days for the dairy farmer and with $30 in our jeans, we set off again. We went past the Bay of Fundy at low tide and down the western shore to Halifax, where we stayed just long enough for Danny to visit his girlfriend. It was only then I found out she was married to a Chinese restraunteur and had borne 2 of his children. What a set-up!

The next day we set out on the Bedford Highway up the Eastern Shore to Danny's home in Beaver Harbour, where I met his family. We spent the next few days traveling around to such places as Sheet Harbour, Musquidobid and many other fishing and pulpwood settlements whose names I don't recall, then back to Halifax and the girlfriend. Danny's sisters allowed us to stay with them—over the protests of one's husband—in their little house on Melville Cove, just off the Bedford Highway.

We had a deadline to meet! We had to turn ourselves in to the army before the end of 21 days, at which point AWOL becomes desertion, a crime then still punishable by 20 years in jail. The upset brother-in-law helped us out a little. On our last visit to Danny's girl before going back, he called the Shore Patrol. They caught me in the hallway and Danny in Doris's bed. We spent the next 3 days scrubbing floors and doing rifle drill with wooden rifles at the Naval Detention Barracks in Dartmouth, across the harbour from Halifax. My first taste of jail ended with the arrival of an NCO from Ontario to escort us back to Camp Borden. Strangely, he removed our handcuffs as soon as we were on the train and asked us to swear we would not try to escape. We quickly agreed. When we stopped over for 6 hours in Montreal, he told us to go see the city and be back before the train left. What we didn't realize until later was that this was a test to see if we could be trusted not to take off again. We passed the test and I'm sure that it had a lot to do with the mild sentence of 28 days detention handed us by the Regimental Sergeant Major after our hearing.

Back to floor scrubbing and double time in #12 Detention Barracks—Cassidy's Castle—so named for its commander, Colonel Mike Cassidy, who ruled the place with an iron fist.

I had had enough of the army. At my hearing I had told the RSM that I had just turned 15 and wanted out. After 14 days of detention, they received confirmation of my age and I was freed. I was still technically in the army when I said goodbye to Danny and boarded a train for Calgary. A week later I received an honourable discharge and a standing invitation to return when I was old enough. One officer even shook my hand and complimented me on finishing basic training. He told me I looked every bit a Canadian soldier. The flattery was lost on me for I had decided that having seen what the weapons of war, in the hands of young men, could do, to never, never willingly set foot on another army base as long as I lived. Almighty God was indeed with me that day, though I would not know it for many years. I was sent back to Peace River on the train. I had only my new uniform, a small bag, $23 and a longing to see the girl I left behind. Bad timing. She had found another beau and although she was happy to see me and wanted to pick up where we left off, I had a hard time forgiving her. Finally, she won out but our relationship wasn't the same after that. I learned (the hard way), that I could not expect a girl to be true while I went off, God only knew where and for how long. We continued to see each other, off and on, for the next 8 months or so.

In late August I met and went to work for a prosperous, young farmer named John Hansen. John owned the most land and the best equipment in the area of Brownvale, Alberta. He taught me to operate huge tractors and combines and I also ran the local road grader. I left at snowfall with a promise to return I the spring. I spent the winter running around from job to job, town to town. I worked in the oilfields twice, once as 'dozer operator' and once as a "swamper" on a big truck. I had at least 5 other jobs as well. I would work for a month or so and then spend a week at Granny's with Thelma. They had moved in to Manning so Thelma could go to High School. And so passed the winter.

In April, I went back to work for John Hansen and he proceeded to teach me everything he knew about farming. I learned to paint, drive a grain truck, repair machinery and buildings and all the other things that make a farmer resourceful and self-sufficient. This knowledge would stand me in good stead for the rest of my life, and I have many times recalled his iron will to survive when I was in difficult circumstances. There was, of course, a catch. It became obvious to me that I was the son he would never have. His wife had lost the ability to have children with the birth of their 14-year-old daughter. She was a pretty girl, just like her mother and I liked them both very much, but when it became plain that John was hoping that I would stay on until she grew up, I beat a selfish, hasty retreat. I packed my clothes and left, barely saying goodbye—an act that I regret to this day. I should at least have gone back and told John how good I felt about being considered good enough for his girl, but I just couldn't do it. That was the first time that a flaw in my nature caused me heartache. It would happen many times in the years to come, hurting me and others deeply.

For the next 8 or 9 months I traveled around the three Prairie Provinces. I helped harvest a bumper crop for two drought poor brothers near Bindloss, Alberta, who paid me double during the drunken party that followed. I rode a freight train for the first time, got caught and spent 3 days in jail. I worked at anything and everything. I acquired (illegally) a driver's license and from then on I did very little labor work; I had graduated to sit-down jobs—trucks, crawler tractors, graders and all kinds of mobile equipment. If it had a seat, engine and wheels or tracks I could operate it and did. So continued my life of feast and famine. Big pay checks and big hang-overs. Happily banging about from pillar to post, I worked my way back, in the spring of 1953, to Dawson Creek BC. The Alaska Highway seemed like a magnet for me, always drawing me back.

CHAPTER 9

"A NORTHLAND ROMANCE"

Then came my second experience with the army; Word came down from Maintenance Headquarters at Truch, BC (mile 201) that the Department of National Defence (DND) was hiring truck drivers and machine operators for a "roving crew" to rebuild and resurface short stretches of the Southern section of the highway that summer. Off I went to Truch Mountain, where I was hired as a combination truck driver and cat operator for the princely sum of $2.50 per hour-$20 per 8 hr. day. Prosperity at last! Good money and time to spend it after work. It was the first job at which I worked less than 12 hours a day, and in that lonely north country the only place to socialize were the army canteens at each successive camp. I was good at my job and I loved it. I must have hauled and bulldozed a million yards of gravel that summer. It seldom rained but when it did it would wash out parts of the highway and we had to divert water, replace culverts and rebuild sections of roadbed. But I didn't mind because there was no mud. No mud! The significance of this fact can only be grasped by those people who have been raised on the Canadian prairie where the cycle of slogging through mud, choking in dust, freezing in 3 feet of snow and then living with mud again in the spring is as ingrained as their character and language. To finally be in a place where there was no mud was like being in a different world.

On 9 July, 1953, my 18th birthday, we reached mile 300 on the Alaska Highway. The post office called it Fort Nelson. There was no fort, of course, never had been. Just a Hudson's Bay Co store, a gas station and a converted army H-hut, laughingly referred to as a hotel. It did have some rooms for rent, but only because it was a requirement for having a retail beer license. No hotel accommodations, no liquor license. It served a rather large area. The DND maintenance camp (where I stayed) was just up the road but the army camp proper was at mile 295, across the Musqwa River. The airport and Air force Base were 11 miles to the northeast. To round it off, there was an Indian settlement about 20 miles upstream on the Nelson River. There was also the constant highway stream of trucks, cars, trailers and jeeps traveling between the lower 48 states and Alaska. So, in spite of its humble appearance, Fort Nelson was quite a lively place, especially on the weekends. There was a little café beside the "hotel", and it was there that I met the girl who would one day change my life. Kay Lowe was a beautiful fun-loving creature who simply mesmerized me the first time she served me apple pie and coffee. It wasn't love at first sight, but close to it.

Now, given my negative attitude toward the female gender at the time, it must have been the Lord himself who brought us together again and again on those long, hot summer evenings. She had been born and raised in Bonanza, Alberta, about 100 miles west of my home. Her folks were homesteaders like mine and we had many things in common. I told her all about my gypsy life so far, and as it turned out, that was a mistake! My crew stayed in that camp for the best part of a month after I met her, but I don't recall much other than spending every hour that I could with Kay. She seemed to have cast a spell over me, and though I tried not to get involved, I couldn't seem to put her in the same slot in my mind where I had learned to file almost every other girl I had met.

Inevitably, the day came for the crew to move on, but only to Summit Lake, Mile 392 at the top of Steamboat Mountain. From there I could hitchhike to Fort Nelson each weekend, and so I got to know Kay better and better. Then we moved to Muncho Lake, mile 456 and it was no longer easy to catch a ride back to see my girl. Two weeks passed and then it began to rain. Torrents of rain high in the mountains soon became a flood that threatened to wash out a mile of highway at the mouth of a huge gravel wash. We worked night and day, sleeping only when exhausted and eating right on the machines. It lasted for 2 weeks and then it took another week to rebuild the road and shore up the diversion dikes. Only then could I think of visiting my wonderful, earth-bound angel.

I arrived in town on the 29th of August, a date I would never forget. Kay was gone!!!! Up to Alaska, some said. Others suggested she might have gone to see her folks in Bonanza. No one really knew. No letter at the post office, no word with friends—nothing! I was heartbroken. I felt like a fool. I had been dreaming about starting a new life with her. I felt that at last I had found someone "different", only to have let her get away. I couldn't even stay in town; I went back to Muncho Lake and drank myself into oblivion. I worked in a hung-over daze the next week and got drunk again on the weekend. I was bad company, and everyone left me alone. The next Monday, I was sent to perform an amazing task, one that brought me out of the fog and into the real world again. It gave me the "out" that I had been looking for so I could leave the area and the places and people that reminded me of Kay.

The DND, in its infinite wisdom, had decided to change lubricant suppliers. Esso-Extra oil and grease from a Canadian company would replace the RPM Delo left behind in large quantities by the US army, when it turned over the highway to Canada. The warehouse at Muncho Lake had been cleared out to make room for the new supplies. The old stock, consisting of over 100 barrels of RPM Delo, was piled outside. The Commandant told me to bury it all because he saw it as a greasy eyesore. I saw it as easy money. I carefully pretended to dig a great hole and bury the lot. Of course, I only buried the bent, broken and leaking containers. The new, unopened and undamaged ones I carefully hid in the bush along with 2 12" x 3" timbers from the bridge repair compound. I then quit my job and headed back to Dawson Creek.

Upon reaching "Mile 0", I quickly found an out-of-work trucker to go to mile 456 and retrieve my loot for $250. Two days later, in the middle of the night, we loaded all the truck could carry and headed back to mile 0. After much haggling and running around, I sold the booty to a contractor for $275. Net proceeds—$25. Big deal! I wasn't about to go back for the rest. (do you suppose the trucker and the contractor were in cahoots???).

CHAPTER 10

"LEARNING LIFE'S LESSONS"

I took a job with a grain farmer named Blaine Pierce while I waited for my last cheque from the DND. We harvested wheat for 3 weeks. When we finished, he asked me to stay on for another month of "fall work", but I wanted to put reminders of Kay behind me, so with a grand total of $750, I headed for Prince George in the interior of BC.

I landed a job pressing pants in a dry-cleaning plant and took a room across the street in the Europe Hotel. Living "in style" for the first time in my life, I quickly fell in with a pair of itinerant, alcoholic accountants who were there to audit the books of an obscure contractor who was in Dutch with Revenue Canada. We had some memorable, if disgusting, times over the next 2 months. My "stake" dwindled away to nothing and I finally got fired from my job. The accountants finished their work about the same time and after one last party, returned to Vancouver to find more work. I had developed an aversion to big cities, so I headed west to the mining and timber country in the Skeena River Basin.

Working at one short-lived job after another, I eventually came to Terrace, BC, in the "big tree country", one of the most beautiful spots I have ever seen. I found a job as an apprentice in an auto-body shop and decided to settle down. The job paid well because most of the men who came to town were loggers who wanted to work in the outdoors, and logging was the lifeblood of the town. Great logs, one per 60ft. truck, came down from the mountain slopes to fill a huge yard by the rail siding. Once each day, a special train called "The Logger", (what else?) was loaded by special machines for the 90-mile trip to Port Edward on the Pacific coast. The highway to the Kitimat power project was just being slashed, so the town was full of men earning good money. There were also many women attracted to the boom economy, so the bars and gambling dens did a roaring business. This, of course, was a great temptation for me but for the first time in my life I restrained myself. I felt that if I could fit in here it would be a good place to spend the rest of my days. But, as always, trouble was waiting. This time it came in the form of a married woman with 2 children. I will leave the details to the reader's imagination, but the net result was a threat to my life and I couldn't really blame the guy. It was an impossible situation, so I packed my few belongings, said goodbye to the my beautiful mountain valley and moved on.

First, I went to Port Edward, with its amazing 72", 60-mile, wooden, fresh-water pipeline, the only large wooden pipeline I would ever see. By coincidence, my older brother, Bob, had helped construct this wonder 10 years before, and had brought home pictures for all to see. On to Prince Rupert, where it rained and rained, then back up-river to a mining camp to drive a truck. We hauled great loads of limestone, blasted from a mountainside, some 18 miles to a rail siding. The road was the worst I had ever seen. We alternately waded through 3 feet of soupy mud on the forest floor then clung to cliff sides on a rocky, narrow trail. I worked only until the first payday and moved on. Hazelton, with its Red Rose gold mine, the deepest and hottest in Canada. Smithers, where I almost froze to death. Housten, Burns Lake, Vanderhoof and finally, back to Prince George.

It was then that my life took an ugly turn. Falling in with 2 itinerant workers like myself and a half crippled squatter/moon-shiner, I split cordwood by day and drank by night until the market ran out. The others began shoplifting and stealing to make money for food and booze, and encouraged me to do the same. At first, I shied away and took a side trip to the south. I visited Quesnel, Cache Creek, Litton, 100 Mile House and all the other famous towns of the "Caribou Gold Rush". In Williams Lake, I found a job in an auto-body shop but was fired after a week for drinking. I went to work I in a sawmill, but injured a groin muscle the first day and was sent to hospital in Kamloops for 3 weeks. Upon my discharge from hospital, I collected my pay and compensation cheque—total $300, which I promptly lost in 15 minutes at a poker table. The experience made me physically ill and I have never gambled since. I went back to Prince George and began a short life of crime with my cohorts. The end came in a darkened alley as we went through the bags of a tourist family, looking for something of value to sell. We never had a chance. The Mounties walked up on us from both sides, and all we could do was give up.

Sentenced to 2 months in jail for theft, we were sent to Okalla Provincial Jail in Burnaby, just outside Vancouver.

Suddenly, it was spring! I worked for a few days planting potatoes and peas with about 20 other prisoners, then I was sent to the dairy barn and did "easy time" for the rest of my stay. With time off for good behaviour, we spent a total of 6 weeks in jail. When released, they gave us each a bus ticket to Prince George. I had no intention of staying in the city, but I used the ticket anyway, just to get out of Vancouver.

After one last party with my "friends", I left. I had very little money but I managed to buy a pair of second-hand shoes and some summer clothing. With my last $5 bill I bought a train ticket east to McBride. Then I began hitch-hiking—on the wrong side of the river! When the road ran out, I guessed I was about 40 miles west of Tete-Jean-Cache Where I hoped there would be a bridge across the river. On the other hand, I might be able to catch a freight out of BC. Fat chance! The rail line over which I was now walking was almost dead level and all the trains were going too fast. So I walked and cursed the surveyor who had laid it out and walked some more. It wasn't boring, as every half mile or so there was a trestle. I would "listen to the rail" and then cross at a run. I had more than one close call. This was the main line of the CNR, so there was a lot of traffic. So I walked, and slept in the bush, and walked some more.

At last, I came to a trail beside the track, and a few miles further on, to a store—and the bridge!—That wonderful, bare-timbered, creaking, old bridge. I almost got down and kissed it! I spent 20 cents on two chocolate bars, (the first food I had eaten in 3 days), and crossed the river. Spotting a cabin that was obviously lived in, I first knocked and then, hoping the owner would not return soon, I walked in. I helped myself to some oatmeal and, seeing the hay filled barn, I determined to have a good rest. Snug and warm in the hay, I slept like a dead man—and almost became one!

I awakened to the sound of a shouting female voice and the sight of an old woman standing over me with a pitchfork! The lady of the house had returned, and I was in trouble again. She made me come into the house and explain myself, and after hearing my story, she laughed and forgave me. She had seen me at the store the night before and felt sorry for me. When she returned to the house, she knew I had been there and finally found me in the barn. But, containing herself, she let me sleep until 10 o'clock the next morning, before confronting me. I stayed there for 3 days, doing chores and splitting wood to repay her kindness. When I left, she apologized for not having any money to pay me, but gave me a heavy, woollen work shirt that had belonged to her late husband. I left, saddened and happy at the same time. Saddened by the woman's lonely life, and happy because I was now on the proper road. It was barely wide enough for two cars to meet, but to me it was a grand highway. It ran past beautiful Mt. Robson and really became a highway in Jasper National Park. It followed the route of the present day Yellow-head Highway and connected to Alberta Highway #16 East. In a few days, I was back in the mud and dust of the prairies.

CHAPTER 11

"EASTWARD HO!"

I spent the next five months working on farms in Alberta and Saskatchewan. I stayed out of trouble, but I drank at every opportunity. Work, eat, sleep and drink. Very little else. I finally wound up in Winnipeg, broke and cold. There is no place on earth colder than the corner of Portage Avenue and Main Street in downtown Winnipeg. I stayed mostly at The Salvation Army mission, when I was sober enough to gain admittance, and ate 2 meals a day in their kitchen. Good Ol' Sallyanne. All my life, since I was about 9 and they gave us all winter clothing, I have had nothing but praise for their work on our country's skid rows. I went to them for help many times when I was young, and was never turned down. When things were the worst and all else failed, you could depend on The Salvation Army for the necessities of life. May God bless everyone who has worked for or given to this fine organization.

I finally tired of this parasitic life and cast about for an alternative. There was no work to be had—no use even looking. I had almost convinced myself to start heading west when I learned, via the grapevine, that I could get free, warm passage the other direction. A train loaded with live cattle left the CPR yards every night for Toronto. Insurance regulations required the cattle brokers to send along a "herdsman" to deal with the loose cattle in the event of a train wreck. It was a foolish rule, as 1 man could not possibly keep track of 2000 steers in the Northern Ontario bush in the dead of winter. The brokers obviously thought so too, for they sent along anyone who wanted to go. The pay was nothing but a free ride to Toronto in a warm caboose. So, after packing some food and waiting my turn (there was a line-up), I started off, once more, for Ontario. Any place was better than Winnipeg that winter.

After two days and nights, we arrived at White River, Ontario, on the north shore of Lake Superior. There the cattle had to be unloaded and fed. This had nothing to do with me—I was just baggage. While having a beer at the local hotel, I heard about the "Geko" gold strike just 150 miles to the northwest. A railroad spur was being built from Hemlo, 60 miles west of White River, into the mine site. There were 14 different construction camps and I was sure there would be a machine for me to operate if I could just get there. I immediately abandoned my trip to southern Ontario and my dubious obligation to the cattle broker, and began making plans to go to the gold fields.

The town of White River was unique in that it was completely isolated—no road in or out. There were only 15 miles of streets and roads, but surprisingly, there were about 50 cars and pickups. There was even a gas station where I worked for 2 weeks to earn enough for a sleeping bag and some warm work clothes.

I stepped down from the day-coach at the Hemlo siding at 10:00 P.M. to find it to be the only building there, and it was closing for the night. The stationmaster pointed out the new roadbed leading off into the snow and said I'd have to "hoof it". 4 hours later, I arrived at the first camp, tired, wet and cold. The camp attendant found me a bunk, and next morning, I hired on as a 'dozer operator. At first, I just pushed blasted rock over the end of the fill. After 2 weeks they gave me a new D-8 'dozer and sent me ahead to "pioneer" the new rock cuts. It was a good job but it had one flaw—there was plenty of booze to be had from the commissary. I behaved myself for 2 months, then got drunk and got fired. I cannot explain to you why I went back to White River. I guess the booze wreaked my logic. Anyway, that's where I went, telling myself I would just have one party and buy a ticket to Calgary or somewhere west of Winnipeg. I had the party all right,—for 2 weeks! I finally ran out of money and, of course, out of friends. Broke and hung-over, I was grasping for straws when I heard the CPR railroad had almost shut down because of a record snowfall at Chapleau, the next Divisional Point east of White River. They needed men to clear the yards. I took the offer of a free ride, free room and board (in old Pullman cars) and $1.50 per hour and shoveled snow for 12 hours a day for the next 10 days. What an experience! There must have been 200 of us. Germans, Italians, Portuguese, French Canadians, bums, derelicts, and a few guys like me who soon found one another. Our little group of ten or twelve were all penniless but somehow managed to scrape together enough each day for tobacco and a jug of wine. When all the snow was finally cleared, we were each given a wooden medallion the shape of a 50 cent piece with our number on it. This little disc got us first-class passage to Sudbury and our pay when we got there.

I spent the rest of the winter in Sudbury, working on a new reduction mill in Copper Cliff. And drinking—always drinking. How I survived the winter among those hard drinking, hard fighting miners is still a wonder to me. I thought I was pretty tough in those days, but every second or third man I met on the street was bigger and tougher than me, not to mention mean. But I survived, and in the spring I headed back west—on a freight train. The Trans-Canada Highway had not yet been completed, so I rode a boxcar to Fort William (now Thunder Bay). Then, I hitchhiked my way west to the prairies. I spent the summer working and traveling around Saskatchewan and Alberta and at first snowfall I found myself in Irma, Alberta. My only reason for stopping there was to get a room for the night and a few beers, but it was to become the most decisive turning point in my life! I would not know it for many years, but Almighty God had taken my life firmly into His hands.

CHAPTER 12

"DOODLE-BUGGING"—(AGAIN)

In the beer-parlour, I met a trio of men who seemed just as intent as I upon milking the very last drop of pleasure from life. They drank and laughed and carried on just like I did. Sensing a kindred spirit, they welcomed me to their table, and, as it turned out, into their lives. Hughie, Dewy and Dale; Operator, Party Chief and Shooter, respectively, for Party #1, Maritime Geophysical Exploration Co. LTD. These were the key men of a "doodle-bug" crew, working a small oil prospect in the area. When they found out I had seismic experience, I was even more welcome. I was hired on the spot to run the line crew, who laid out and picked up the cables and geophones, and whom I had yet to meet.

Next morning, cold and red-eyed, we assembled in the lobby where I met the crew. Fine young farm boys, working at their first jobs. They were a little wary of me at first, but by that night, we were moulded together by the bond of hard work, well done. And so it went, for the next 3 weeks; work hard and fast all day, and drink as much as possible before the bar closed. Dewey Armaneau, our boss, was a sort of entrepreneur cum con-artist, and kept us all supplied with the necessities, including cash advances. He juggled the client (Oil Co.), the bank and his credit cards to keep the wheels turning.

We finished the prospect at Irma 2 weeks ahead of schedule, and the owner informed us that our next prospect was at Truch Mountain, B.C., Mile 201 on the Alaska Highway. Memories, long buried, came flooding back. Memories of my fleeting angel, Kay Lowe. She was probably married now, with a couple of kids. But, no use weeping about the past, I had a job to do—a good job. I was being promoted to "shooter" as well. Dale Hewittson was leaving to head up a second party and my experience put me in line for his job.

Truch Mountain was different, to say the least. Rough, rocky lines on steep mountainsides gave us many a hair-raising experience as we worked our hearts out trying to produce barely half as much completed work each day as we had back on the flat prairie in Alberta.

It was on this prospect that my friendship with Hughie Wilson, our operator, began to mature. We worked well together and enjoyed the same things, including booze. It was Hughie who first told me that I was considered an alcoholic by most who knew me, including him. Because I knew he was sincere in his concern for me, for the first time I began to consider the possibility. It would take me 13 more years to admit it to the rest of world, but I knew in my heart that he was right. I was, and still am, an alcoholic. I was addicted to the stuff—one drink was too much and a thousand were not enough. I began to worry about it—when I was sober—and began trying various ways to cut down and become a "social drinker". Life without any booze at all was unthinkable. I felt I was on the brink of disaster. There had to be more to life than work and booze, but I felt that whatever there was must be far out of my reach. I began to brood and wonder if life was worth living at all. Even when Dewy told us that our next job was at Fort Nelson, I couldn't muster much enthusiasm. In fact, the day we left, I had drank so much that we had a heated argument as to whether I would drive the shooting truck, loaded with dynamite, on the highway. It was some trip, with many stops to check equipment (and to check on me, I learned later), but we finally arrived at the town site at 11:00 P.M., and parked in front of the new Avonlea Hotel.

CHAPTER 13

"OLD LOVE—NEW LOVE"

I crawled out of my truck and entered a whole new life. For there, behind the check-in desk, sat Kay!!! My mind froze! I was caught between the bitterness I had felt all these years and a feeling of happiness and delight just seeing her there. As a thousand thoughts crashed around in my head, I blundered through the job of checking in, hardly saying hello. I tried desperately not to let her see the effect our unexpected meeting was having on me. We spoke only briefly, and since I was dead tired, I trudged upstairs to sleep. Morning wasn't much better as we shambled in for breakfast. There was Kay, happily serving the crew bacon and eggs from the restaurant kitchen, where she seemed to be in charge. We finally left for work, but I though of little else all day. I had a lot of trouble deciding what to do about her, but she took matters into her own hands that night after supper. She invited me to sit down with her and her friends, and it wasn't long before we were at least talking freely to one another.

Over the next few days, the story un-ravelled. While I had thought she had run out on me more than 2 years before, she had thought the same of me. I had missed 3 weekends without coming t visit her at Mile 300, and that, combined with what she knew about my habits, was enough to convince her I would not be back. She couldn't stay either and took off for Alaska to put me out of her mind. We had probably passed within a few feet of each other on the highway between Mile 300 and Mile 456, Muncho Lake. Our old feelings came rushing back, and we lost no time catching up. I was happy again; I had found my wonderful Kay and little else mattered.

This happened just before Xmas and it was the best Xmas gift I had ever had. We laughed together, ate together and on one occasion, worked together. New Year's Day 1956, with a new, keen interest in my job, I offered to go out and pre-load some shot-holes for the next day's work. I invited Kay along, and we bounced and banged our way over some 50 miles of bulldozed line, loaded the holes, and bounced our way back to town. Kay was so sore the next day she could hardly walk. She discovered that the bouncing seat had worn a hole in her new slacks. But nothing could dampen our enthusiasm for living life together. We talked of getting married, even though neither one of us had anything that would not fit in a suitcase.

The winter flew by, and eventually, it was almost time for the crew to move again. I had made up my mind not to leave with them, but Hughie Wilson and I had one last adventure. Our gas tanks were sabotaged one night and the next day (about 2:30) the gas lines began to freeze. We soon discovered the problem—snow in the gas—but darkness prevented proper repairs that day. We had one vehicle, the ½ ton surveyor's truck that would run. After a short discussion, Hughie and I shoved (literally) the rest of the crew into the small cab and sent them on their way to town. Then someone was to return for us. It was the best thing to do, under the circumstances, as Hughie and I were older and more experienced than the rest. We began to walk as the temperature dropped from -10 to -20 F. The first 2 hours weren't bad, but as that stretched to 3 and 4, and we saw no returning headlights, we began to worry. Many things could have happened, such as the survey truck suffering the same fate as the others, or breaking down, or getting stuck on the icy hills. But, no use to conjecture, we continued to walk through the freezing night. Now, however, each time we passed a shot-point, we looked for the waxed paper dynamite wrappings cast aside during our work. We soon had it stuffed everywhere in our clothes and were looking for a good place to start a fire, when, abut 10:00 PM, we saw a light. Not the bright lights of a vehicle, but a dim, hesitant light, not far ahead and off to the right. As we walked closer, we discovered we had come to the Indian village on the Nelson River. We decided to ask for shelter until help arrived.

This proved to be a more difficult task than expected. Of the four inhabitants of the house, none could, or would, speak English. We finally made our needs known and were allowed to sit on the floor with them. There was no furniture—none! A stove and some cardboard boxes in one corner—that was it! Every half hour or so one of them would go outside and bring in more wood for the stove. Hughie and I took turns watching at the window watching for a truck from town. At about 1:30 AM or vigil was rewarded. We rushed out, thanking our hosts, and flagged down what proved to be our survey truck. We were happy, angry, tired and hungry all at the same time. As we rode back to town, the driver told us what had happened.

Harry Tchere, our assistant party chief, new to the North Country, made what could have been a deadly error. He reasoned that Hughie and I were quite capable of thawing out at least one gas line in the dark and therefore, there was no need to rescue us. He sent the men to supper and waited for our return. Then Kay found out and all hell broke loose! She gave Harry such a tongue lashing that he finally sent someone after us. Hughie and I were pretty mad but since the prospect was almost finished, we decided to let it alone.

When the crew moved out I drew my pay, said goodbye to Hughie and the boys, and went to work for a man named 'Nat Smith, a local legend. He had been in the north since the Highway was built and owned several businesses, including a service station/truck stop and a 5 ton Ford transport truck. He had a contract to haul High-Velocity-Gelatine from the warehouse at Mile 308 to locations far out into the muskeg where it would be used by helicopter crews during the summer. Some of these spots were 150 miles distant, requiring me to drive for up to 50 hours in second and third gear over the rough trails. Kay accompanied me on many of these trips. The big truck, loaded with up to 8 tons of high explosives did not bounce like the shooting truck had so we had many long conversations about everything imaginable. She was smart as a whip and had a good sense of humour, so she was very easy to talk to. Thus began a practice that has kept us both interested and talking for over 55 years.

It was on one such trip that I made the single, most important decision of my life. It had been a particularly hard trip. I had lost my whole load on an icy hill when I "spun out" and slid backward into a stump. After reloading by hand in the middle of the night (5 hours for 14,000 lbs. of Geo-gel), I reached my destination to find no "push-out" for my normal square stack. I was forced to pile it two boxes wide on one side of the trail so that vehicles could pass. On the way back, I neglected to check the temperature at the bottom of the Nelson River hill, and because it was warm, (April 5th) and I had not "chained up", the truck spun out about ½ way up and slid backward, right over the bank! It came to rest at such a steep angle that I had to shut the motor down. There I was, 30 miles from home and because it was so late in the season, the likelihood of help coming along was very slim. I had only one option—I must "boomer" my way out! There was just one stout tree across the road, and linking both of my tie-down chains together, I secured one end to the tree and the other to the front axel. Then, using both of my boomers, I began the slow, backbreaking chore. Placing one boomer over the other and snapping it tight, to gain about 2 inches with each pull, I slowly pulled the truck back onto the road. Then, I put the skid-chains on and proceeded up the hill, sore and played out. I never forgot again! I was just glad the truck was empty—I might still be there!

So—as I started to tell you many sentences ago, I had a lot of time to think about Kay. Kay and I, to be more precise. Having been against marriage for so long, it was very difficult to consider it now. I was 20 years old and Kay was 24. I somehow knew that if I did not marry her now, I would lose her—forever! After much agonizing, I decided that life without her, again, would be unbearable. So, like it or not, when I reached town, I would ask her to marry me. She said "YES" at 9:30 in the morning of 5 April 1956 and by 4:00 in the afternoon the deed was done!

What a wedding it was! We had to borrow a ring, ask our closest neighbours to stand up for us, and get the Government Agent to perform the ceremony! By chance (or was God arranging things?), Kay's brother, Jack, a long-haul trucker, rolled into town and stayed for the momentous event. He looked me over pretty well, but in the end he wished us well, as did all who knew us. We had a rousing party, and then went to the tiniest honeymoon home anyone ever had. Barely 10 x 12 feet, it had a bed, a cook-stove right beside it, a "stove-pipe" propane heater and one chair. A very humble beginning, but we loved it as we did each other. God had given me the most wonderful gift possible and I wasn't even sure He existed. But I knew, somehow, that my life was no longer on the brink of disaster. I was to be given another chance.

PART II

CHAPTER 1

"A NEW BEGINNING"

Fort Nelson was not a good place for a workingman in the summer. The oilfield virtually shuts down and it was fairly certain the DND would not rehire me. Besides, I wanted to start out fresh in a new place with my new bride. I contacted a farmer I had worked for the previous fall and he sent us two bus tickets. Away we went to Neilburg, Saskatchewan—as happy as 2 young people in love can be. We moved into the little house in the farmer's yard and tried to settle down. I drove a tractor in the field and Kay worked part time for the farmer's wife for vegetables, eggs and milk. We had no transportation, but at first that didn't matter because we had each other. We also had a great little garden, which we hauled water to every day.

Then a sort of discontent set in. I made only $140 per month, and after buying the few necessities of life there wasn't much left. If I got drunk on Saturday night, there wasn't any left. We needed clothes and entertainment and we despaired of ever having a car. Finally, we allowed ourselves to be led down the garden path into debt. The farmer (who shall remain nameless) suggested that we take out a loan with Household Finance Corp. We thought that might be the answer to our immediate problems. We took out a loan for $250. I will never forget that first step into financial bondage. It led to a way of life that all newly married couples should avoid like the plague. But, we reasoned, everyone else did it so it must be the thing to do. Before long, the money was gone and other than a few new clothes, I cannot recall gaining one thing from it, except a monthly payment of $17.50. I soon realized the farmer was playing a game with us but I hated to admit my foolishness to my new wife—so I began planning to move on. It seems dear old Mrs. Kent was not perfect after all. She, and everyone else, for that matter, had neglected to teach me basic logic. I was still learning life's lessons the hard way!

I must pause here to tell you of a brush with death I had that summer. The farmer, his brother and I set out one day to get a tree planter to put in little saplings for windbreaks. The planter weighed no more than 100 lbs., but since it was too wet to work in the fields, it was party time—for all of us. Many hours and many beers later, as we were returning home in the dark, we broke over a hill at 80 MPH, (which was as fast as the old Ford pickup would go) and spotted—too late—a deeply rutted section of road across a very big, and very deep slough. We hit the ruts, bounced twice and landed nose first in the water. We were lying on the driver's side and of course, that door would not open. I was sitting next to the passenger door, on the "up" side and it wouldn't open either. When I rolled the window down, water rushed in and filled the cab! Believe it or not, I was the last one out. Those two farmers panicked and stampeded right over me, their heavy boots almost knocking me senseless! In spite of my injuries, I managed to get out and get to shore. If I'd had the strength, I would have thrown them both back in! By morning, we had gotten a tractor to pull the truck out, but in the meantime, about a dozen bottles of beer had floated out. We had to borrow a boat from the owner of the tractor to retrieve them. It was a big joke afterward, but a new pattern of drinking was beginning to form in my life. I was becoming a "binge" drinker. I would stay sober for weeks at a time, then drink until all the money was gone. Satan has many traps and snares at his disposal, and alcohol is one of the worst.

I finally got a chance at a job running a grader for the Rural Municipality of Manitou Lake. We quit the farm with 2 days notice, said goodbye to our little garden, and left. Some would say "out of the frying pan into the fire"! Most of the roads in the district were not gravelled and had to be maintained on a regular basis. 12 hours a day, 6 days a week, if it rained, my pay ($2.35 per hour) was docked. On the other hand, we didn't have any rent to pay. The fuel trailer and shop were set up to include bachelor quarters—a ¾ bed and two-burner, Coleman gas camp stove—that's all. Looking back, I can hardly believe we lived in such miserable conditions.

The trailer was 8' x 14' and we shared it with grader parts, extra cutting edges, tools grease and oil. We got our water from various sloughs and creeks as we moved along. Kay packed the water, cooked, washed clothes (on a scrub-board) and kept us alive and happy. She even managed to preserve about 100 quarts of peaches, plums, saskatoons and wild strawberries. An evening out was usually her riding on the grader with me as I put in extra hours to increase the size of my paycheque. There were few opportunities to go to town (on the grader) and still fewer to drink, so we had a little money to spare for a change. I honed my skills on the grader. It was my favourite among all the machines I had operated. It allowed me to leave a perfect road behind me, and I quickly realized that as long as I could do that, I would easily find summer work.

As summer gave way to winter I was laid off for the season. The only one kept over the winter was the foreman, and I was not yet ready for that. So we brought all of our belongings, including the preserves, to the little town of Wilkie, Saskatchewan. There we rented a little two-room suite above a hardware store and dug in for the prairie winter. The landlord, a very kind and generous sort, also had one-room suites for rent and we moved back and forth, up and down the hall, as our fortunes rose and fell. I was drawing unemployment insurance but it was not enough to live on ($17.40 a week) so I worked 4 hours a day at the local dry-cleaning plant and Kay worked part-time at the town's only restaurant. In spite of all this we were happy and I didn't drink as much. Kay hated my drinking by this time and tried her best to make me stop. When I was sober, she stuck with me through good times and bad, putting up with conditions that would have wrecked almost any marriage.

I must pause here to recount a friendship that we sort of drifted into that winter. An old Swedish couple moved in just down the hall from us. Having just sold their farm, they were as starved for company as we were. We soon became strongly attached to them. Our only entertainment was cards, which, for the lack of anything else to do, we played for hours on end; sometimes losing track of day and night, playing until 5:00 in the morning and sleeping until 2:00 in the afternoon. We helped each other get through that awful winter, and I still regret not keeping in touch with them after we moved away in the spring.

Spring did come, at long last, and I landed a much better job running a grader for the Rural Municipality of Perdue, 40 miles west of Saskatoon. We moved to Perdue and rented a furnished duplex. As the pay was much better, we were soon able to buy our first transportation—a 1950 ½ ton Ford pickup. What a difference it made! What freedom we suddenly had! We finally began to live life on the same level as the people around us. It should have been the first step on the way to a secure and happy life. But my human nature (which was Satan's nature) would have none of it. I drank at every opportunity and finally, in July, after a drunken weekend spree, I quite my job.

CHAPTER 2

"PRAIRIE STORMS"

Kay hated the prairie and the thunderstorms. I remember spending a whole night in the truck because of the lightening. She was also lonesome for home and her folks. When I came home one afternoon and proposed that we pack up and return to Dawson Creek, she had us ready to go in two hours. The truck loaded high with our worldly possessions, and the cat and dog crowded in with us, we set off for the Peace River country, almost 1000 miles away. 6 rainy, muddy days later we arrived in Dawn Creek, BC. Wet, discouraged and almost broke, we began the task of rebuilding our lives.

But it was not to be. The next 5 years were a mélange of working, loving, drinking and trouble. I worked for the B.A. Oil Company as a tanker truck driver for almost a year, but was finally fired for my drinking habits. I lost the pickup to the finance company; lost most of my friends and blamed it all on the hand life had dealt me. I could always get a job running a grader in the summer, but in the winter, the only job I could get was cutting lines for seismograph exploration in the sub-arctic, where I was almost killed on several occasions. My closest brush with death came when the D7 "cat" I was operating broke through the ice on a northern lake. We always worked in pairs and only the quick action of my partner saved me. It was crazy! I was risking my life daily for $3.75 per hour! I drank most of my money and Kay had to keep our home and pay the bills on her own wages.

In the summer I was usually found in a road construction camp somewhere in Alberta or North-eastern BC. I became an expert blade-man, and thus was able to hold down a job and drink too, whereas a man of lesser abilities would have been fired. So one of the truly good aspects of my character became my enemy, leading me further and further toward the brink of disaster.

CHAPTER 3

"MUD, GRAVEL, PULP-WOOD AND PIGS"

One rainy day, in the middle of a surfacing job at Grande Prairie, Alberta, I became embroiled in a drunken dispute over the Company's accounting practices and quit the best job I had had up to that time. I took Kay with me and hired on with another construction company at Eaglesham, some 150 miles away. After a week, I realized, though an alcoholic haze, that I had made a very bad choice. Kay and I had a fight over it and I left. I told the boss to give her my pay-cheque and I left the only person I loved in this whole wretched world. It took about 2 months of drinking, working and loneliness to make me understand that I could not live without her. I then "borrowed" my current employer's pickup (I had sold our car) and a 45-gallon barrel of gas. Then, with all my clothes and a gallon of cheap wine, I headed back toward home, about 900 miles away. I had to stop 80 miles short of my goal at Beaverlodge, Alberta when the gas and wine ran out at the same time. After a 12-hour sleep, I had sense enough to phone Kay. She came to my rescue—again.

She talked me into turning myself in to the local R.C.M.P. Two days later, in Edmonton, a kindly judge gave me a one-year suspended sentence. He also put me on "the Indian list", which meant that I could not drink legally for 12 months. I hitchhiked 100 miles west to Edson, where I hired on as a grader-finisher—with the same company I had sold the DND's oil and grease to some 8 to 10 years before!

No one recognized me, however, and I settled down to sober up and clear my mind. I phoned Kay and begged her to come to me. I convinced her I had stopped drinking and promised never to start again. Again she came back to me and we were happy again for a while. I drank no alcohol for the next six months. Winter came and shut down the construction job, and after a period of unemployment, a friend and I bought a chain saw and began cutting pulp-wood. It was a hard way to make a living, but I was home every night with Kay and all was well.

Then, for no valid reason that I can recall, I got drunk and stayed that way for a week. Once started again, the old pattern returned. Kay begged, cajoled and threatened, but I kept on for all the rest of the winter and into summer.

In late July 1961 I met and struck a deal with a hog farmer near Cochrane, Alberta. I would help him with his pigs and do the fieldwork for a wage and raise 20 pigs of my own. Kay came down to cook for us and all went well for a while. We bought a ½ ton IHC pickup and we had wheels again. Harry Webb was a nice man, and we got along just fine. The money wasn't great but we had no expenses. The prospect of selling our hogs for a profit in April made the immediate future look bright. Then, in March, I started boozing again and Harry cancelled our agreement. I took our pigs to market under-weight and we had to move again. It was too early for any road construction, so I phoned a farmer in Swift Current, Saskatchewan and got a job to get us through the next month or so.

That's the way it worked out. I hauled grain, stayed sober and helped put in the crop, then we returned to Calgary. Kay wanted to go back to Dawson Creek, but I was convinced we would be better off in the city. I remember the incident well because I was really afraid of losing her at this point. I knew that life without her would not be worth living. I also felt that only in the city would I be able to get the help I needed to stop drinking forever. Although this did prove to be true, it would take another 6 long years.

CHAPTER 4

"CITY SLICKERS"

Overcoming my long aversion to big cities, we settled down in a third floor room of an old house for $30 a month. We shared the bathroom on the floor below us with 2 other couples. It was as humble a home as could be found, but it had the redeeming features of being close to a bus stop and a 20-minute walk from downtown. I still remember the address—523—18th Avenue SW. This was the first of at least 20 places we would live in over the next 6 years. We moved up and we moved down, according to our financial fortunes. Whenever I stayed sober, our living standard and quality of dwelling rose to a fairly comfortable level. When I drank, down we went again.

Through all the ups and downs, Kay held a steady job and continued to be the only anchor I had. I worked as a grader finisher in the summer, and with the exception of 1 y ear, spent the winters in the sub-arctic cutting seismograph lines. Through it all, the high quality of my work, (of which I was quite proud) kept me on the payroll when I would otherwise have been jobless and starving.

I must pause here to recount the winter of 1964-65. Instead of going to the Arctic, as was my habit, I decided to take a less dangerous job closer to home. I became the shooter for a small company doing deep-well velocity surveys for oil and potash exploration companies. This involved a seismograph instrument being lowered to the bottom of the borehole while the drilling rig was still in place. Then we would raise the instrument 50-100ft. at a time. Each time the "tool" stopped I would fire a charge of high explosive in a shallow hole near the wellhead. The observer's (my boss's) instruments would record the resulting vibrations from the tool on a strip of photographic paper. These records, when correlated with other data from the well, yielded much valuable information for the client and much repeat business for us. We traveled far and wide, from Rainbow Lake in north-western Alberta to Virden in southern Manitoba, but I did get to be home once a week or so.

In early November, I had the only accident in my long association with high explosives. We were shooting a potash exploration well near Willow Bunch in south-eastern Saskatchewan. We got started late, had a few hold-ups and consequently, found ourselves in the dark with only vehicle headlights to help us. As shooter, I should have forced a halt to operations until daylight, but with a million dollars worth of equipment standing idle, not to mention wages for three crews of men, I was badgered into finishing the hole. On our last shot, I set the charge (luckily it was only 5/8 lb. of geo-gel) at 40 feet and left my helper to retrieve the loading poles. He dropped them, as usual, right at the shot hole and retreated to my position. We forgot 2 rules that I should have checked, but didn't. First, he neglected to check the spear hole with his hand to make sure the charge was not still attached (it was). Then, upon returning to my side, he turned to face the shot hole—another no-no. When I fired the charge he got a face full of frozen clay particles, injuring his right eye. It could have been much worse. My truck was carrying 700 lbs. of HE, which, if set off, would have wiped out everyone on the lease, some 15 or so men.

We immediately rushed my helper to the nearest hospital and as soon as we were assured he would be all right, I was sent hurrying back to the lease. The boss had only just then informed me that he had no permit to operate in Saskatchewan. So it fell on me to get our trucks and explosives across the border into Alberta before the RCMP began an investigation. They could still get to us personally, but they could not seize our vehicles or equipment. That was the thinking at the time. Whether it was true in practice, I never learned.

It was quite a night. We drove almost 300 miles on secondary roads to cross the border before dawn. We arrived back at the main highway and a motel at 10 AM. I had not slept for 72 hours. I just lay down on the floor—muddy clothes and all—and stayed there for 6 hours. On the long drive back to Calgary, I promised myself I would never break the rules regarding high explosives again.

It was a very timely decision, for the next week we got a contract to shoot some wells in The Yukon and the Northwest Territories. All were inaccessible by road, and therefore, we could not get the requisite shot holes drilled, except at great expense. So we had to use "shaped" charges on the surface and mobile instruments. Shaped charges meant liquid explosives.

Not nitro-glycerine per se, but nitro-methane and ethelyne-diamine mixed onsite just before firing. Extremely unstable in it's final form. (I mixed it with a wooden spoon). With this stuff, we followed the rules! A blast wall (of snow) had to be pushed up by the "cat" to protect the rig workers and ourselves from the tremendous force of the blast. We shot 3 wells over a period of 6 days, flying out of Shell Oil's base camp in the Peel River Gorge to the Peel Plateau in the Yukon, and to Arctic Red River N.W.T. The flying part was just as hairy as the explosives. The aircraft were always overloaded and the airstrips were short. When we left for Norman Wells on our way home aboard an old, overloaded DC-3, the pilot had to fly up the Peel Gorge for about 3 miles to gain enough altitude to turn out. I think my fingerprints are still on that jump seat!

One day, Kay and I were carefully transferring some of the nitro-methane (relatively stable on it's own), from a barrel to gallon-sized gas cans in the back of our car. As we were doing this, a sudden snow squall enveloped us and we didn't see or hear the locomotive, which was about to pass us, until the engineer blew the whistle for a nearby crossing. I know, you probably think I made this up! But I didn't—honest! It was a scene straight out of a "Keystone Cops" movie. To say we were scared would be the understatement of the century. I did many things that winter that I would never, never do again.

The drinking continued unabated. I lost my job and for a year or so I stumbled from one job to another, sometimes trying to stay sober, but mostly just despairing of having any life other than that of an alcoholic. I couldn't live without it. For a while I just lived from day to day, bottle to bottle, fully expecting to be killed in an accident or die from my own excesses. I respected no one except Kay; the thought of her hurting would make me cry sometimes, but if I could get enough to drink, even that was blotted from my mind. She stayed with me, never losing hope for long. God himself only knows why.

Finally, our possessions gone,—no car, no furniture, few clothes, no phone—we moved into a single, furnished basement room in a 50 year-old house on 13th avenue near 8th street SW. I remember it clearly because the means of my rehabilitation lay only 2 blocks away. I didn't know it then, but God was about to intervene in our lives on that dingy semi-slum street in the spring of 1968.

PART III

CHAPTER 1

"REBUILDING"

There is no way to describe on paper what it is like for a drunk to sober up without the hope of ever having another drink. Despair, hopelessness, fear, pain—both real and imagined—sanity slipping away, not being able to separate fact from fallacy, nightmare from reality, right from wrong or love from hate. All these words and phrases have been used by those who have written before me, and all of them combined cannot fully portray the experience of an alcoholic's final withdrawal from booze.

God, in His unfathomed love and mercy, using my beloved Kay as His instrument, dragged me, kicking and screaming, back from the brink of self-destruction. Kay, still trying to reason with me after all these years, after all the heartaches and tears, finally convinced me that I needed professional help. I had tried AA, an organization that I respect and honour to this day, but somehow the program, which has saved hundreds of thousands over the years, just wouldn't work for me. This time, we decided to go to AADAC (the Alberta Alcohol and Drug

Abuse Commission), and we found the nearest counselling center barely 300 yards away. I was introduced to Antabuse. Under close supervision, I swallowed one of the little white tablets each day, building up a very effective allergy to alcohol. The method was simple—keep antabuse in your bloodstream and one drink would send you into convulsions. I hungered and yearned for booze, but I feared the drastic consequences of taking a drink.

Let me dispel any thought from your mind that kicking alcohol was the result of any courage or strength on my part. It was not! Kay was the one with the courage, strength and love; the councillors were the ones with the logic, the will and the means. I supplied only my momentary consent, and within a week, would have cheerfully withdrawn it. But antabuse is like booze, it has a long-lasting effect. You must stop taking it for 3 to 5 days in order to drink without getting sick. I made a pact with Kay; she would give me my pill each morning because she loved me and I would swallow it because I loved her! I was finally back on the course I had set when I asked her to marry me. As the days and weeks passed and I stayed away from my old buddies and my old haunts I began to find a little pride in just being ME! With Kay's love and God's love, I was able to withdraw from the vague, hazy, confused and totally illogical world of excessive drinking.

It would be nice to say at this point that, all my troubles behind me, I lived happily ever after. Such, of course, was not the case. Although I had set down a heavy burden, the battle was not won. The years of drinking had instilled habits and faults in my character that would take many years to root out. But I had survived, our marriage had survived and our love for each other had survived. I thank God for giving Kay to me and helping her through the terrible, unhappy times that I caused her. I thank Him for rescuing the tattered remnant of my being and making life worth living again.

While my rehabilitation gained momentum, I searched out and found a job completely outside my former field—supervising night-time office cleaning crews all over the city. A menial job to be sure, but now with my whole paycheque coming home, added to Kay's, life began to improve at once. In the spring, I took a job operating heavy road-building machinery for The Municipal District of Rocky View, and spent the summer earning good money and coming home every night. I was also home o the weekends. It was a summer to remember. We moved out of our basement hovel and into a beautiful hi-rise. My confidence returning, we struck out boldly and bought a car, then a new car, and then a second new car. This was a 1970 Cougar, a beautiful white and red dream machine. I worked long, hard hours and soon we were able to buy our first, very modest house. It seemed that the nightmares were behind us. We had nowhere to go but up. We began to make contact with our families again. To my very great surprise, they all welcomed me back into the fold. One even said, "Good for you, Dick we knew you would kick it someday". That winter, I again went to the Sub-Arctic to cut line, but this time I made sure I went to a "dry camp" where booze was not allowed. I had my paycheques sent to Kay and when I came home in April, Kay presented me with my first bankbook. Dick Hutton with a bank account—amazing! We took a week off and then I set out in search of a good, year-round job.

CHAPTER 2

"AS GOOD (AND AS BAD) AS IT GETS

I chanced to see an ad for a machine operator in The Calgary Herald by Ace Construction, lots of hours and top pay. Intrigued, I drove to their office. I had no idea what the job entailed, and I almost turned around and left when their sign declared that they were in the business of power line construction. But, having driven all the way across the city I went inside and asked to see the boss.

I was taken to the president's office and offered coffee. It was strange surroundings for me. I was used to men in work clothes. This guy wore a three-piece suit. He grilled me for half an hour about my experience, both with machines and the Far North. It seemed they were branching out into Arctic airstrip construction and needed a point man to get them started. It was an interesting and challenging opportunity. After phoning Kay for her opinion, I signed a contract.

On 19 May, a senior company executive and I headed for Yellowknife, N.W.T., where we took delivery of a new D-6 Caterpillar tractor. It came with a winch, dozer, cab and a set of "gin-poles", all disassembled for shipping. On 24 May, we loaded everything onto a C-130 Hercules aircraft. I bid goodbye the company representative and was soon flying high over the Arctic circle and halfway to the North Pole. 7 hours later, we landed in the middle of the musk-ox game preserve on Bathurst Island in the High Arctic. We were greeted by two cat-skinners who helped me unload and assemble my machine. I found that my D-6 was replacing an old D-8 that was so worn out that it was only good for dragging the airstrip. I would not see darkness again for a month, as the sun just went round and round in the sky, doing crazy things to my biological clock. I slept and ate at odd times of the day and worked as many hours as possible ploughing snow for a huge, new campsite. I was supposed to work until 15 July, when they would send in a relief operator and fly me out for a month's rest but something happened to change all that.

On 28 June, I was about 10 hours into a long shift on the machine and thinking about shutting down for the day. I stopped to smoke a cigarette, and as I mentally weighed the progress of the project, the cigarette dropped from between my fingers. Instinct, born of many years of operating a "cat" in the bush, took over. There are many openings in the deck of a cat through which something as small as a cigarette could fall, and waiting below was a "stump-pan" filled with moss, sticks and grass soaked with oil and diesel fuel. A firetrap, just waiting for a spark! I quickly bent over, my hand darting to catch the cigarette before it was too late!

I don't remember whether I caught it or not, for at that instant a blinding pain shot through my spinal column. I found out later that the quick movement plus fatigue had caused a small muscle in my back to rupture. I should, at this point, tell you that the fire hazard I feared did not exist. This machine, never having worked in the bush, was squeaky clean, stump-pan and all. I held back tears as I managed to sit up straight. I slowly drove the machine to the bunkhouse, and with the help of the 2 men within, I managed to get down and inside to a bunk. I have never felt as helpless and alone as I did that day. I couldn't move without excruciating pain. The others got the radio warmed up and after much trial and error, managed to convey my plight to base camp at Resolute Bay on a neighbouring island. The weather was bad for flying. It was not stormy but the rising fog became an overcast at about 300 feet.

I should pause here to explain that in the High Arctic a compass is useless due to the proximity of the magnetic pole, which moves around and at that time was very near to Bathurst Island. Thus, the only means of navigation available at the time were dead reckoning by the sun, which is risky at best, and following the coastlines of the islands and the straights in between. With the low overcast this latter method posed some problems. Finally, the famous Weldy Phipps (his call letters were W.W.P., or in radio parlance—Whiskey, Whiskey, Poppa) decided to take the risk and fly in to get me. I was carried to his plane and strapped into the co-pilot's seat and off we went at an altitude of about 200 feet. Pretty hairy, but I hurt so much I did not care!

It was during this short flight that I saw a sight that few men are privileged to see! So amazing was it, that for about

20 minutes, I almost forgot about the pain. Seals! Thousands of them! It was whelping time and the female seals were up on the ice flows to give birth to their young, which do not immediately swim. There must have been 2000 mother seals along that narrow strip of water, stretching for about 15 miles. As they heard the approach of the Twin Otter (a relatively quiet aircraft), they rolled off their flows into the sea, leaving their pups behind. What an amazing experience!

We finally reached Resolute Bay, where I went through a series of tests by the District Nurse to determine if my injury was genuine and not just a ruse to get passage south. At last she signed the order that would get me to medical attention in Calgary. I was put aboard an old DC-4 in a stretcher tied to the deck for the 14-hour, droning trip to civilization.

I must mention that while I was in Resolute Bay awaiting transport, Queen Elisabeth II paid a visit to the little community. I managed to see her from a distance but didn't get to shake her hand as most of the men did. She spent about 4 hours visiting the Inuit village while Prince Phillip flew even further north to a drilling rig on the north coast of Elsmere Island. Under different circumstances it might have been a pleasant afternoon, but the pain in my back was such that I moved only when necessary.

Once back in Calgary, in the hands of my doctor, my back began to heal but I noticed that something else was wrong. I couldn't regain my usual happy attitude. My natural enthusiasm for life was gone. I chalked it up to the long weeks of pain and worry and went back to the Islands for a second 4 week shift.

Now I became certain that something was terribly wrong; I couldn't sleep except when exhausted, had little appetite and I was badly depressed. I took my turn on the machine but I didn't talk to anyone unless I had to. I noticed, too, that I had lost my ability to resist fear. I began to avoid even mildly dangerous situations, and the slightest thing made me tremble. I was in sorry condition when the shift finished and I was able to fly home. I quit my job and began a year-long search for an answer to my problem.

I sank deeper and deeper into depression as the days and weeks passed, and winter came with a vengeance. It got so bad that Kay could not leave me alone, so she quit her job too and we applied for welfare. We lost our beautiful car to the finance company, and with our last $165 we bought a 1957 Volkswagen "Beetle", the toughest little car I've ever driven. It got us through the winter and even took us to Dawson Creek once—German Sheppard, cat and all. The speedometer finally flew to pieces, having gone around too many times, but still the car kept going.

That winter was probably the worst time we had spent since our marriage. Only the bingo games kept us same. We played every night, just for something to do. Kay won often enough to keep us going. Most of the time, I sat at home and read. I was withdrawn, fearful and totally lacking in enthusiasm. The prospect of working on a grader in the summer filled me with trepidation. We had declared personal bankruptcy to keep the bill collectors off our backs and, living on welfare, we managed to keep our house and the "Beetle". The world was becoming a sad place for me and I was thinking more and more of suicide.

Kay never lost her smile but I knew, inside, she was hurting for me. I guess God was hurting for me too, because it was then, for the first time in my life, that I became conscious of His existence.

I had subscribed to a magazine called "The Plain Truth", whose editor was the President of The Worldwide Church of God. In its' pages I seemed to find strength and hope, and I read and re-read every issue. I began to listen to his broadcasts on TV and radio. His name was Herbert W. Armstrong, and he spoke with urgent authority on the existence and power of God.

It was early in the spring of 1971 that God chose to rescue me from my plight, steering me along a long and tortuous course that led, at last, to victory. Passed from one doctor to another, I finally wound up in the office of Dr. Kazi Islam, a son of India and a psychological genius. He worked and talked with me daily for a couple of weeks, trying this remedy and that. I seemed to get a little better only to fall back after each effort. Suddenly, one day as I answered his interminable questions, his eyes lit up and he said "I know what is wrong"! He gave me a little orange-brown pill and a glass of water to wash it down and told me to return the next day. I woke the next morning feeling somewhat better, and when I went back to his office he gave me another pill and said, "Come back tomorrow". When I awoke next day, I thought I had been cured! For the first time in about 10 months, I felt like my old self—or at least I thought I did. I felt better and better as the days passed and the dosage increased. I had not realized how far down I had been! My life had been given back to me, and I got down on my knees and thanked God for the first time in my life. I have never doubted His existence or power since that day.

Author's Note: *The exact cause of my depression was not pinpointed until the summer of 2005 (see Epilogue). Dehydration of all things, was at least the main contributor! Since the Arctic snow was polluted so badly, I had been getting by on coffee, which, in itself, is dehydrating! Who knew????*

CHAPTER 3

"THE MAKING OF A CHRISTIAN"

That summer I returned to highway construction for a while, but feeling the need to be home every night, I finally took a job with a developer building and grading lanes in a new sub-division. For the next 2 years I worked at this job and we began to rebuild our lives again. It was during this time that we were baptized into the World-wide Church of God. I'll never forget the date—December 31 1973. I knew now that we could handle anything this world had in store for us. I began to search the pages of my Bible to "prove all things" as Jesus had exhorted us to do. I learned (and Kay with me) that wealth, happiness and worldly possessions were not the most valuable things in life. They could be had and much more, but first we were to seek the Kingdom of God. As Jesus put it, SEEK YE FIRST THE KINGDOM OF GOD AND ALL THESE OTHER THINGS WILL BE ADDED UNTO YOU. Such has been the case ever since. In good times and tragic times, our faith has not failed us, and, as the reader will see, we have overcome difficulties and trials that, without the knowledge that God was with us, would surely have broken our spirits. His strength never fails, and His Son intercedes for us daily.

And so began our walk with God. He fed us milk at first, because He knew we were not ready for meat. As the weeks and months passed we formed a bond with Mr. Richard Wilding, pastor of the Calgary church. We became friends, and for the first time, I began to trust in people—God's people. They were not perfect, as I had expected them to be. They were just like us—trying to be perfect. And as I reflected upon that fact, I slowly began to understand what God's love was all about. He loved us before we knew Him, and He loved us now in spite of our shortcomings. We had but to believe to receive His Grace, through faith in Jesus, His Christ, and The Good News (Gospel), which He brought to us. What an amazing revelation! Not the heavy handed, wrathful God I had imagined, and indeed had been taught about, but a kind and loving God who suffered with us the results of our sins, and rejoiced with us when we made one small improvement in our lives! As one man put it, "it just gets better and better"!

About this time, and I'm sure, at God's direction, we first came in contact with the courier business. We had tried our hand at business but not knowing our way and having no formal training, we faltered and failed. However, determined to work for ourselves instead of others, we soon found an opening. We became driver-owners (commissioned contractors) for what was then a small local delivery service. For 4 years, we rushed around town, delivering letters, small packages, dentures and liquor. We charged $1.00 to $12 for letters and packages and $2.00 to $16 for liquor and we prospered! We made more money than I had ever made running a job or a machine on construction! We had learned the principal of "tithing" and it worked just like magic. If we paid our tithe faithfully, we prospered; if we held back and spent it on something we "needed", we stumbled. It worked the same as the principle of Trust in God. As long as we trusted in Him our way was smoothed before us; the things we worried about never happened. When we gave in to fear and distrust and used our own "wisdom", we paid the price. However, having access to all this new power did not make us perfect, of course. We had, and still have lessons to learn, and such is the heart of Man, that even when he knows the right way, the pulls of the flesh and his own natural vanity and greed will still trip him up.

We prospered to the point that we were able to take our first real holiday. We kept the Feast of Tabernacles with other members of the church at Penticton, BC. What a week it was! Driving 30 miles, twice a day in our rented car to worship, fellowship and feast (literally) with God's people. Our money ran out before our time did so we missed the last 2 days, but it was one holiday we will never forget. Hearing and seeing Mr. Armstrong and his son, Garner Ted was especially gratifying to us. They knew so much about God and the Bible, and we knew so little. Although, in later years, they fell from the grace of the church, I am sure they never fell from The Grace of God. God will not fail to reward them for bringing so many into His Light. We kept the Feast Of Tabernacles for several years with The Worldwide Church of God, traveling once more to Penticton (we stayed the whole 8 days that time) and once to St. Petersburg, Florida. We talk about it still. Those first heady years among God's people gave us a whole new way of life.

CHAPTER 4

"ROLLER-COASTER"

We worked in the courier business until 1977, when I became involved in landscaping and general contracting. We had, until then, employed a full-time housekeeper, but upon leaving the courier business, it was decided that Kay would stay at home and we moved to the country. This proved to be a good move. We lived more cheaply and were better able to handle the ups and downs of contracting. I soon found that I could learn and make money at the same time. On estimating a new project, I tried to stay away from firm quotes and instead work for cost plus 10%. This worked out well for both contractor and owner and I was not in danger of losing money. I was soon doing everything from a new sets of steps to 30ft high retaining walls. I did all the design and forming myself and hired people for the heavy work. It seemed that I had found my life-long calling. But we were not yet through with the courier business or, as it turned out, with booze.

I had "fallen off the wagon" for short periods but not like this. I became weary and depressed at the end of an especially hard season, and began smoking and drinking again. Kay left in desperation and I was on my own for 2 weeks—sober one day, drunk the next. Even a visit from Mr. Wilding did nothing to change my course. Fortunately, two things happened at the same time. I ran out of money and a friend (from the church) called me to see if I would help him out of a jam! He owned a share in a fledgling courier service (Apis Courier LTD) that was in danger of collapse and wanted me to come and get it back on track—company car and all.

Broke, hung-over and dispirited, I went through the first week in a daze. Finally, Kay returned and things started getting better. The many problems the new company faced were mostly small ones, but taken together, they were life threatening. I implemented some very strict rules (over the manager's objections) and things began to improve at once. I was finally able to make peace with Pat Gladys, the manager, and as the winter passed, we all became friends. Kay was brought in as Office Manager and we all began to make some money. Then the partners began feuding over the shares I had been promised and I finally resigned and began my own service—Super courier LTD.

I must admit, at this point, that starting my own courier service was nothing short of an attempt to "show them all" how it ought to be done. With Kay still managing Apis Courier, our interests were split and I was doomed from the start. My new partner and I argued constantly and after 6 months I reluctantly sold her my shares and that was the end of that.

I returned to contracting. I also returned to the Church. And right away, predictably, things began to improve. Kay finally quit Apis too, and we moved to a condominium owned by my sister, Pearl. Again, we prospered. I worked hard and the jobs came in by the dozen. I incorporated under the name of Flying Scotchman Contractors LTD. after the famous train. I applied God's principals in every aspect of the business, and we again "kept The Feast" in Penticton, BC in October. I worked all winter that year (mostly cement work and repairs) and because there were so few contractors working, I made more money than ever. As spring approached, I was getting tired and Kay was getting sick of staying at home, so we hatched the idea of "The Pixies". We felt that Calgary was ready for a well-run, top-notch courier service with well-trained, uniformed driver-owners. A big step up from the rag-tag people already on the streets.

We incorporated, with my niece, Phyllis Harvey, under the name of Pixie Management LTD. Kay and I also registered the trade name, "The Pixies", but under our personal names. In the light of subsequent events, I am sure we were guided by God. Several months later, as we grew to 6 or 7 contractors on the road, we were approached by another small operator to merge our two companies—which we did—and which was almost the end of The Pixies. With the help of a crooked lawyer, our new partner gained complete ownership of Pixie Management LTD., and we were left with shares in a paper company with no value at all. This came to light just after I had sold my contracting business and had my first heart attack!

I felt so helpless in the hospital. Kay wrestled with the problem for several days before telling me, which, of course, was only good sense considering my condition. With the help of a friend at AGT and a good, honest lawyer we put together a plan to relocate our operation and re-incorporate under the name of "Pixie Courier LTD" and retained the trade name "The Pixies", which was already becoming well known. We also retained the customers and contractors of both original operations. We moved on a Sunday to a single room across the street from Baldy's Wood, owned by my brother-in-law, Dick (Baldy) Whittaker. Now, convalescing at home, I spent all day Friday calling all our customers to advise them of our new phone number. As this was taking place, our "partner" allowed his guilty conscience to keep him away. When he finally phoned the old number and got no answer, he suspected the worst. When he did find us it was too late and his rage was unprintable. Our new lawyer was also very clever and he made sure we did nothing illegal so no matter how much our former partner wailed and gnashed his teeth, there was nothing he could do! Once again, we had been rescued from the brink of disaster!

We never looked back after that. "The Pixies" prospered in the face of recession, management errors and very stiff competition. Learning as we went, we again practiced biblical principals in all aspects of our operation. We began attending the Seventh Day Adventist church because, as a now reconfirmed smoker, I was no longer welcome in The World-Wide Church of God. Our expulsion, I'm sure, was a "calculated risk" on the part of our new pastor to help me quit smoking. However, when I could not comply, he had to carry out his threat. So began a period of wandering. We were not lost, but when The Church broke up because of family bickering, we sort of drifted between the splinters of the Seventh-Day movement. After some years of such drifting, we finally found our way back to the original church. Now reorganized under the new name of "The United Church Of God", it follows, almost to the letter, the original teachings of Herbert W. Armstrong.

Mr. Armstrong was the first of many people I have come to know who began a study of The Bible with the sole purpose of discrediting it, only to find himself unable to disbelieve the truth and logic contained therein. He was also the first person who described love in language that I could understand. "Real love", he said, "is an outgoing concern for someone else that is equal to, or greater than, ones' concern for ones' self". Since hearing that, no other interpretation of love has quite satisfied me. He also preached: "don't believe me, I'm just a man—take up your Bible and read it for yourself! Prove every word!" He believed in a "Wonderful World Tomorrow", and so do I. The Church he founded has had many setbacks, but although it has been presided over by imperfect people, it is based on the truth of the Bible as he discerned it.

The next spring, on a cold, wet afternoon, I found that my feet and hands were growing numb. I had just gotten over a bout of the flu, and we thought my heart was acting up. Kay rushed me to emergency at Foothills General Hospital, by which time the numbness had risen to my knees and elbows. A long and painful examination ensued. My heart was fine. My circulation was fine. It was only my nerves that seemed to be affected. Finally, after a desperate phone conversation with the head of the neurology department, it was decided I had "Guilliam Barres' Syndrome" a condition brought on by the body's reaction to influenza and for which there was no known cure. It would either kill me, or I would survive. All they could do was make me as comfortable as possible, and wait.

For the first 10 days, I got steadily worse, and finally, I could move only my hands (with support) and I could still talk, after a fashion. All the rest of my voluntary muscles had ceased to function. Now the question loomed; would it spread to my semi-voluntary muscles and stop my breathing? A tangle of tubes, gauges and breathing apparatus had been installed beside my bed and, worst of all, an emergency tracheotomy device (complete with insertion knife) had been clipped to my pillow, in case I stopped breathing without warning!

Through all this I was surprisingly (to myself) calm. I knew I might die, but it didn't bother me. I felt that I had come to terms with my Creator and I just left everything in his hands. He had further use for me on this earth, apparently, because on the 14th day, I began to recover. Once more, I was being snatched back from the brink of death.

My recovery was going to take forever. At least 6 weeks, maybe more. Things that most people daily take for granted—talking, writing, sitting up, bathing—all seemed desperately out of my reach. The nerves serving my muscles had lost their memories and had to learn all over again. Walking was the toughest, and I worked on it the hardest. I could not abide a wheelchair and I was determined not to be bound to one. I could move every part of my legs and feet on the exercise table, but I couldn't walk—I didn't know how! Finally I was helped to the parallel bars and began to shuffle back and forth. Then I mastered pushing my wheelchair and, 2 days later, walked with a cane all the way from my room to the gym. My 20-year-old therapist was aghast. Where did I get the cane? Why was I pushing so hard? Did I not know I had a right to be sick? I took exception to this last, and finally, she had to admit she was just as happy as I was. Between us, we had shortened the normal rehabilitation period to 5 days. It is easy to pray in a hospital, especially when you know you could leave in a box, but I learned a couple of lessons I'll never forget. 1): no matter how badly you are off, someone else is suffering more (as in the case of the 17 year old beauty I met in the gym who had lost her left leg far above the knee); and 2): with Jesus at your side, you can face anything.

CHAPTER 5

"THE LITTLE CHURCH"

Since leaving the World Wide Church Of God, we had cast about for an alternative. We had many times passed by a little church on Center St. that proclaimed itself to be The Church of God (7th day). One day, on impulse, we stopped and took a closer look at their freshly painted sign. It said all were welcome and gave us the pastor's phone number. We called and were invited to attend services the following Saturday. Little did we know how much this encounter would influence our lives.

The new (to us) congregation proved to be a very friendly, close knit group. Small in numbers, large in faith. Fundamentalist, to be sure, with no added frills. Just a rock-solid belief in the Bible as it is written and in the Gospel as Jesus and His apostles taught it. Their basic doctrines were contained in a small booklet and there were no added traditions. It seemed almost to good to be true, but as the weeks and months passed, our scepticism dwindled. We actively looked for faults and inconsistencies, but to no avail. No one pushed us to become “members”. Our baptism (by immersion), into the World-Wide Church was accepted as valid, and we finally came to the conclusion that here, at last, was the true spirit and embodiment of the gospel of Jesus Christ, reflected in an association of human beings.

We had tithed our income to the church we attended since 1973 and we continued to do the same here, but the results seemed different. We began to prosper, as we never had before. Not just in money, but in all other ways as well. We finally had friends that we didn't have to hide anything from. Other blessings continued to rain down upon us. Our marriage, which had suffered so many indignities on my account in the past, blossomed and bloomed with happiness and contentment. Our business relations improved and mellowed. Our entire outlook on life took on a whole new meaning. We began to relax and trust more in God and His promises, and less in our own wisdom and logic. We got more pleasure out of everything we did, and the burden of guilt that I had carried for so long, became lighter—almost non-existent. The future—the real future, now seemed firmly within our grasp. We even visited what some call “Paradise on Earth”—Hawaii!

CHAPTER 6

"THE GLORY YEARS"

Just a few short years before, it would have seemed unthinkable for a Hutton to vacation in Hawaii, but after my sister Pearl had blazed the way, earning her Master's degree in education at the university there, we just had to go. I had a dozen reasons why we should not spend money in such a fashion, but they were ignored or brushed aside and, one fine spring day we arrived (not unwillingly) at that much talked about spot on the map—Waikiki.

What an experience! We were infected by "the bug" immediately, and like so many before us, began to search for a way to make this our permanent home. We checked out real estate and business possibilities, and even opened a bank account. We were coming back—no doubt about it. Just a matter of selling our business, obtaining a visa and buying a home. We'd work out the pesky details later. And all this after seeing only one island! Our first trip to Wiamia Falls was the clincher. We had never been in a more beautiful spot. The fact that I couldn't stand the heat for too long and spent most of my time in an air-conditioned room or car didn't dampen our enthusiasm. If we had had the means, we would not likely have come back. I couldn't think about anything except living there for the rest of our lives. We came home in high spirits, already planning our next trip.

We went again—the same year—and found that some of the sparkle had worn off, but we still went through the motions of finding the right spot to live. We dreamed and calculated and felt that, having taken a second look, we could safely make the "big decision" when the time was right. And that one phrase, "when the time is right" proved to be the deterring factor.

Back home—the second time—we were able to think rationally and logically. Slowly, (at least for me), we came to the conclusion that; 1) given the fact that we only have 10 to 20 years left in this life, we might just as well live right where we are content with the knowledge that 2) We will soon be living in God's Kingdom, beside which our "island paradise" would pale into insignificance. It was something like leaving the gold nuggets in the creek, and continuing on to the "mother lode". A heart-rending decision, to be sure, but the right one—the enduring one. 20 years is a tiny speck that cannot even be found in the immense span of Eternity and a lush, green island cannot be compared to a city of gold. We still look back and dream, but now it is just that—a beautiful dream. We will stay in the place, and with the people to which God has led us and be content until our change. When Jesus Christ returns, our place, whether island paradise or frozen prairie, will make no difference and will be lost to our remembrance anyway.

CHAPTER 7

"ON THE BRINK AGAIN"

"The Boy From The Bush" has come a long, long way in 75 years. I have seen and lived the best and the worst and just about everything in between. I suppose you could call my experiences the ingredients of wisdom, as this world counts wisdom, but I have come to understand that real wisdom begins with the knowledge of, and belief in, the Word of God. That God and His Christ, Jesus are the wellsprings of wisdom, and that worldly wisdom is but foolishness in comparison. And so, I find myself beginning AGAIN, as I have so many times, a journey into the unknown. But this time I have the advantage—this time I cannot fail. I have the Word of God as my guide, Jesus as my light, and my beautiful Kay as my help and companion. I am "on the brink" again, but not on the brink of disaster, on the brink of Glory! There will be obstacles and trials, of that I am sure, but there will be no turning back. I intend to spend the rest of my life preparing for the return of Jesus, as King of Kings and Lord of Lords. Whether it be in my physical lifetime or after a long sleep, I want to—I must—be ready! I will do such business as is necessary for our health and comfort and I will try to keep us physically and mentally alive. Beyond that, I intend to keep my waking moments open for the absorption of whatever wisdom and Grace I might acquire on this new journey.

At this moment, my darling Kay is indulging in her one luxury—large screen T.V.—Wondering when I will put down my pen and join her. I'll leave you with this line from an old Protestant hymn—"God be with you 'til we meet again".

Yours in the love of Jesus, our King—Dick Hutton

EPILOGUE

(The Last 20 Years)

We now live in a large house in a newer part of Calgary, having moved from Penbrooke in August, 2009. With us is our ever faithful friend, Prescy, her husband, Noel and her three sons, aged 16, 14 and 12. We are comfortable and happy, having gained most of our goals. However, the last 20 years have not been without their trials and tribulations, as you will see.

In December of 1990, while we were living in a in Edgemont, we felt that we could now turn our business over to a manager and take it easy for a change—big mistake. We were not meant to "take it easy" that early in life, and we chose the wrong type of person to run our company. She was overly ambitious and craved independence at any cost, we were to learn (too late).

On New Years Day, 1991, we received a phone call—my older brother, Bob had died from a heart attack, and would be buried on 5 January in Peace River. I left for the place of my birth next morning. I almost made it.

As I drove down the Gruard Hill just south of town, I was hit head-on by a truck traveling on the wrong side of the road. My van crumpled up like a tin can, trapping me inside and knocking me out cold. I awoke just as a fireman forced my door open. I was taken, in great pain, to the hospital where I had been born 55 years before. I was found to have a concussion, 6 broken ribs, a badly dislocated hip, a crushed larynx (I have trouble speaking to this day) and multiple minor injuries and bruises. They re-set my hip, wrapped up my chest with a drain on both sides and pronounced me ready for transport to Calgary. Kay had flown up the night before and accompanied me in the Stars Air Ambulance on the flight south. I was in a "sorry fix" as my Grandfather used to say. For the next month or so we concentrated on my recovery, leaving The Pixies in our manager's hands. I guess you already know what happened next—that's right—our banker stopped cashing our payroll cheques, and when I went to him to protest and he saw the condition I was in, he froze our entire account, effectively putting us out of business. We were pretty angry, but there was nothing left to do but start over—again!

We declared The Pixies and our personal selves bankrupt, and after weeks of legal tap-dancing, we opened a small operation under the trade name of K's Messenger Service and began to regroup. I hired 3 driver-owners and began visiting our former "Pixies" customers. I am not a good sales-man, so it was pretty tough going. Then one of the new driver-owners asked to see me. At first, I thought—more trouble—I could not have been more wrong.

Dennis Remington told me he had some experience in sales and thought he could sell enough new accounts for us to get things rolling again. I took him up on his offer, and so began a friend-ship that has lasted through thick and thin ever since. With his enthusiastic help, we were able to interest a trans-planted Ontario business man in our venture. I had recognized the necessity of having both strong sales and basic business skills plus investment capital in order to build and sustain a healthy, growing service company. We also needed cash to run our daily lives.

We advertised for a partner with capital, business ability and computer experience and found Bruce Bechtel, who has also become a life-long friend.

We "paid out" Kay's bankruptcy and incorporated "K's Messenger Service Ltd." with Kay as President (55%) and Bruce and Dennis sharing 45%. I remained in bankruptcy and Bruce supported the company financially until a law suite against my insurance company played out and they finally settled my claim. I was able to repay Bruce the money he had advanced, take a legal position in the company and settle some long-standing obligations. The combination of enthusiasm, hard work, sound business practices and God's help, I am sure, began paying off and we were able to start planning for proper retirement.

We prospered in everything that we did until December of 1999, when we sold out to one of our strongest competitors. We used the proceeds to buy a small house and fund our long hoped for retirement.—I can here you shouting "HALLELUIA, THEY MADE IT"—But not yet!!

Remember the dehydration ??? Well, it was not through with me yet. I began to have spells of depression again, so bad that I became delusional and could no longer trust myself to drive. I became a burden to Kay instead of a caring husband. I began to think more and more of suicide. Kay's' health was failing because of me. The future leered at us with foul and fetid breath. I finally wound up in the mental ward, where I prayed for the release of death.

As the days passed, Dr. Bhanji, the psychiatrist assigned to me, began experimenting with new drugs and I slowly began to come out of the fog. I improved to the point that they were able to move me to a transitional place called "Care West" beside the Rocky View Hospital. A long drive for Kay to visit me each day, but she never missed—not once! It was here that Dr. Bhanji and others began to put together a history of severe Dehydration. It had started in the Arctic in 1970 where the melted snow water tasted so Awful I could not drink it and substituted it with coffee or beer, both of which are dehydrates. Now, of course, a great deal of damage had been done, some of it irreversible.

Now that things have been artificially balanced, I have regained most of my faculties. I will have to drink 3 times the normal amount for men my age till I die. I will also have to take certain things by mouth that my battered nervous system no longer provides. I feel very fortunate and blessed to be sitting here in my right mind telling you how these last 20 years have been for me and mine.

I have not lost faith in our Creator or His Christ. If anything, it has flourished, and just in the last 2 weeks, I have made contact with the TRUE CHURCH OF GOD !!!!! Yes,—While searching for a book, Mystery Of The Ages, written by Herbert

W. Armstrong, I was led to the Philadelphia Church Of God. I was stunned! God's truth was still out there! Needless to say, I spend most of my time now learning and re-learning the truth about God's soon coming kingdom on THIS EARTH. Walking down the same path that I did in the 70's and the 80's.

I now realize that God has been guiding me for my entire life. First, giving me a curious and understanding mind and an excellent teacher. Then, the kind of experiences that moulded my character into what it is today. It is this character that I must improve and add to as my final days pass by. I will not be lazy in this regard, as I have been in the past. When Jesus returns He must find my hands still holding the plough.

I will be 76 years old this July. I have my beloved Kay at my side. I have made my peace with God and His Christ and I await their good pleasure.—Dick.—19 February, 2011

"PRESCY"

In the summer of 1989, after a couple of bad experiences with short-term housekeepers, we answered an ad in the paper advertising Pilipino domestic workers. We were introduced to several applicants with pictures and all. We chose a young lady with a beautiful smile. And so began our amazing relationship with Prescilla Briones.

Arrangements were made for her to fly to Calgary and she left her island home with $100 in her pocket. We met her (and her smile) at the airport, and in just a few days, established a friendship that has lasted through thick and thin ever since. We were soon calling her "Prescy" and marvelling at how hard she worked and her cheerful disposition. Nothing seemed to faze her. She and Kay hit it off right away and they talked for hours. She is probably the happiest person (besides Kay) that I have ever known. Before long, we realized that we had found a gem and we had better do every thing we could to keep her. Even when our business collapsed and we could no longer pay her, she simply asked if she could take an outside job and continue living with us. We were overwhelmed!

After a few years, she returned to her home to get married. She returned as Prescilla Cabrera, and not long after, realized she was pregnant with the first of 3 boys. Franz was born 8 months later and his father, Noel, came to live with us a short time after that. He found a good job and proceeded to become a very good father. Two more boys, Hanz and Janz, followed at two year intervals. Franz, or Frankie, is now almost 16 and we all live together in a nice house on a quiet street in Woodbine S.W. Calgary. Some have said that it is not good for God's people to live so closely with people of the catholic faith, but Pressy's joyous outlook on life and her patience and faithfulness overcomes all that. We love her and have made her our daughter in every way that counts. May God continue to bless her and her family.

BACHELORS

When I was a boy in the early 1940s, we lived on the very edge of civilization near the little town of Peace River, Alberta. Life in "the bush" was interesting to say the least. We were fascinated by the lonely men who had settled in the area for (as you will see), various, strange reasons. They were a source of wonder to us, and we were welcome company to them. Let me introduce a few of them.

"FRENCHY" LA MERDE: Frenchy, like my Father, was not a farmer, and cleared only enough land to build a huge house of perfectly squared timbers and plant a big garden. He had been a ship-right in Montreal until he killed a man in a fight. He was famous for his feats of strength and his skill with a broad-axe. He worked on various construction projects in the area and walked everywhere he went, as he hated horses. At least once a month he would carry a 100 lb. sack of flour home (13 miles) from town. My Father found him sitting at his table with the remains of his last meal. He had been dead for several days. When no next of kin could be found, my Dad dismantled his house with the idea of rebuilding it for my Mother but she would have none of it, so it became a barn instead. That barn was my Father's pride and joy!

OL' GENDRON: Napoleon Gendron was also from Montreal, where he toiled as a "moulder" in an iron foundry. The first 24 years of his marriage resulted in 18 children. He left them all and the big city for the peace and quiet of the wilderness to pursue his dream of inventing a "perpetual motion" machine. He was assisted in this endeavour by yet another displaced Quebecer, Mr. J.D. Levesque, a prominent merchant in town. J.D. would drive his (always new) Oldsmobile out to the farm almost every Sunday to check on progress. Their "machine" once ran for 2 weeks on two flash-light batteries. Ol' Gendron used to tell us stories about the city with it's street-cars and lights and ships in the harbour. This was all mind-boggling to us, as no one in our district had electricity or phones. Our only entertainment was a wooden, battery-operated radio. I spent many hours listening to that old man and dreaming about someday going to the big city myself.

HARRY LLOYD: Harry was a "remittance man", the nephew of a wealthy English brewer. He had so embarrassed his family in London that they sent him off to Canada with a purse full of money and 50 dollars a month if he would just stay away. He never worked, other than to grow enough barley to keep himself well stocked with beer, and to hunt for deer and moose. He refused to own a car but kept the best pair of riding horses that money could buy. When he was sober, Harry was always looking for a scheme to make money. He was seldom successful, but he once sold all the timber off 160 acres (which he did not own) to the American army. The Police left Harry alone because he never sold one drop of booze, unlike my next subject.

TOBACCO JOHN: John Korwalski had a propensity for chewing and smoking at the same time. He also distilled corn mash and produced the best "moonshine" in the country. It seemed that at least once each winter, the R.C.M.P. would get a complaint about John and "investigate". They never found his "still", and it was rumoured that they left a lot happier than when they arrived. John carried a .45 revolver everywhere he went. One winter night he was shooting mice inside his cabin and in his enthusiasm, put a bullet through his front window. He patched it next day with a shingle on each side and a plough-bolt to hold them there. The neighbours laughed so much he just left it that way. He owned 1 of only 2 cars in the district and he liked to take a jug around to visit the "the boys", as he called the other bachelors, on Sundays when the bars were closed. He used to tell us stories about his young days in Ohio. He also taught us how to spit accurately. He would practice spitting at dandelions for hours, and claimed that a dandelion drenched with tobacco juice would never grow again. He was probably right.

DAVEY COOK: Dave was a Scottish seaman who came to our district to keep from being drafted into the Navy. He and Dad became great friends and they would go out shooting rabbits and sell their pelts to the government for 10 cents each. They could shoot 100 on a good day. The draft board finally caught up to Dave in March of 1945. He gave me his trusty .22 repeating rifle as a parting gift. I practiced shooting at heads of wheat and was soon bringing home enough grouse and prairie chicken to keep us in meat. I was quite proud of my marksmanship. I never saw Dave again but I will never forget him.

SAM HOLT: Sam was the biggest farmer and owned the most work horses in the Roma plain, west of Peace River. My father worked for him from April until October, shoeing the horses and driving them in the fields. Sam (6'2" 220 lbs.) really liked my dad (5'2" 160 lbs.) because my father, a very proud and powerful man, stood up to him. He kept working the farm with horses until 1947, when all his neighbours had been using tractors for years. He used to laugh and say "if I bought a tractor, Joe Hutton and his family would starve to death". He may have been right! My dad used to say "if he had not had me to do all the work HE would have starved to death". Finally, he bought the biggest John Deere tractor on the market and sold all the horses. My dad drove it for one summer and then moved to town and retired.

ERIC BRAE: "Poor Eric", my mother called him. He lived with his parents on a small farm and was so shy it was pitiful. It seemed like every girl over the age of 15 in the district got at least one proposal of marriage from Eric. He was desperate to wed but no one would have him. If he went to a dance, the girls would tease him unmercifully. The last I heard, Eric had stopped going anywhere except to town for groceries. I hope that he eventually found someone to share his life.

FRED DEMETROKOWICH: Fred had come from Russia with his brother John and they settled a mile from each other. Both were very hard workers and good farmers. John married and raised a family while Fred seemed to like his own company. He had a hard time learning English but when he was about 45 years of age, he managed to ask my father if he could marry my sister, Doris. I guess that's the way they did it in the old country. He never talked about it to Doris. It was a complete surprise to her. My father, (on her behalf), politely declined. Fred was a pretty good catch for some one who spoke Russian so he likely married some one after I left home.

AMAZING GRACE

Amazing grace, how sweet the sound
That saved a wretch like me
I once was lost, but now I'm found
Was blind, but now I see.

'Twas grace that taught my heart to fear
And grace that fear relieved
How precious did that grace appear
The hour I first believed.

Through many dangers, toils, and snares
I have already come
'Tis grace has brought me safe thus far
And grace will lead me home.

How sweet the name of Jesus sounds
In a believer's ear
It soothes his sorrows, heals his wounds
And drives away his fear.

Must Jesus bear the cross alone
And all the world go free
No, there's a cross for everyone
And there's a cross for me.

When we've been there ten thousand years
Bright shining as the sun
We've no less days to sing god's praise
Than when we first begun.

CASEY AT THE BAT

By Ernest Lawrence Thayer
Taken From the San Francisco Examiner—June 3, 1888

The outlook wasn't pleasant for the Mudville nine that day;
The score stood four to two, with but one inning more to play,
And then when Cooney died at first, and Barrows did the same,
A pall-like silence fell upon the patrons of the game.

A straggling few got up to go in deep despair. The rest
Clung to that hope which springs eternal in the human breast;
They thought, "If only Casey could but get a whack at that—
We'd put up even money now, with Casey at the bat."

But Flynn preceded Casey, as did also Jimmy Blake,
And the former was a hoodoo, while the latter was a cake;
So upon that stricken multitude grim melancholy sat,
For there seemed but little chance of Casey getting to the bat.

But Flynn let drive a single, to the wonderment of all,
And Blake, the much despised, tore the cover off the ball;
And when the dust had lifted, and men saw what had occurred,
There was Jimmy safe at second and Flynn a-hugging third.

Then from five thousand throats and more there rose a lusty yell;
It rumbled through the valley, it rattled in the dell;
It pounded on the mountain and recoiled upon the flat,
For Casey, mighty Casey, was advancing to the bat.

There was ease in Casey's manner as he stepped into his place;
There was pride in Casey's bearing and a smile lit Casey's face.
And when, responding to the cheers, he lightly doffed his hat,
No stranger in the crowd could doubt twas Casey at the bat

Ten thousand eyes were on him as he rubbed his hands with dirt.
Five thousand tongues applauded when he wiped them on his shirt.
Then while the writhing pitcher ground the ball into his hip,
Defiance flashed in Casey's eye, a sneer curled Casey's lip.

And now the leather-covered sphere came hurtling through the air,
And Casey stood a-watching it in haughty grandeur there.
Close by the sturdy batsman the ball unheeded sped—
"That ain't my style," said Casey. "Strike one!" the umpire said.

From the benches, black with people, there went up a muffled roar,
Like the beating of the storm-waves on a stern and distant shore;
"Kill him! Kill the umpire!" shouted some one on the stand;
And it's likely they'd have killed him had not Casey raised his hand.

With a smile of Christian charity great Casey's visage shone;
He stilled the rising tumult; he bade the game go on;
He signalled to the pitcher, and once more the dun sphere flew;
But Casey still ignored it, and the umpire said "Strike two!"

"Fraud!" cried the maddened thousands, and echo answered "Fraud!"
But one scornful look from Casey and the audience was awed.
They saw his face grow stern and cold, they saw his muscles strain,
And they knew that Casey wouldn't let that ball go by again.

The sneer has fled from Casey's lip, the teeth are clenched in hate;
He pounds with cruel violence his bat upon the plate.
And now the pitcher holds the ball, and now he lets it go,
And now the air is shattered by the force of Casey's blow.

Oh, somewhere in this favoured land the sun is shining bright,
The band is playing somewhere, and somewhere hearts are light,
And somewhere men are laughing, and little children shout;
But there is no joy in Mudville—mighty Casey has struck out.

LEETTLE BATEESE

You bad little boy, not much you care,
How busy you're keepin' your old Grand Pere.
Tryin' to stop you every day,
You chase de hen aroun' de hay,
Why don't you give dem a chance to lay?
Leettle Bateese.

Den out on de fiel', you follow de plow
An' when you tire, you scare de cow,
You sikem de dog 'til she jump de wall,
An' de milk aint good for nutting at all,
An' you'e only five an' a half dis fall.
Leettle Bateese.

Too tire' for sayin' de prayer tonight?
Never mind 'spose be allright.
Say 'em tomorrow—ah, dere he go,
Fast asleep in a minute or so,
An' he say like dat 'til de rooster crow.
Leettle Bateese.

Den he is wake us up, tute suite,
Lookin' for somet'ing more to eat.
Makin' me tink of de long-legged crane,
As soon as he swallow, he's eat again.
It's a wonder y our stommick don't get no pain.
Leettle Bateese.

Look at him layin' dere in bed,
His little brown arm underneet his head.
If he grow lak dat til he's twenty year,
He'll be as strong as Lois Syr,
An' he lick all de voyaguer leavin' here.
Leettle Bateese.

Look at de muscle along his back,
Won't trouble him much for carry pack,
On de long portage, any size canoe,
Der's not much ting dat boy won't do.
For he's got double joint in his body too!
Leettle Bateese.

But Leettle Bateese, please don't forget,
We radder you're stayin' de small boy yet.
So chase de cow, an' make her scare.
And do what you lak wit' your old Grande Pere.
For when you get big fella, he won't be dere.
Leettle Bateese.

Dr. William Henry Drummond—1896—Montreal, Quebec

THE BALLAD OF SALVATION BILL

'Twas in the bleary middle of a hard-boiled arctic night,
I was lonesome as a loon, so if you can,
Imagine my emotions of amazement and delight
When I bumped into that Missionary Man.
He was lying lost and dying in the moon's unholy leer,
And frozen from his toes to finger-tips;
The famished wolf-pack ringed him; but he didn't seem to fear,

As he pressed his ice-bound Bible to his lips.
'Twas the limit of my trap-line, with the cabin miles away,
And every step was like a stab of pain;
But I packed him like a baby, and I nursed him night and day,
'Till I got him back to health and strength again.
So there we were, benighted in the shadow of the Pole,
And he might have proved a priceless little pard,
If he hadn't got to worrying about my blessed soul,
And a-quotin' me the Bible by the yard.

Now there was I, a husky guy, whose god was Nicotine,
With a "coffin-nail" a fixture in my mug;
I rolled them in the pages of a pulp-wood magazine,
And hacked them with my jack-knife from the plug.
For Oh, to know the bliss and glow that good tobacco means,
Just live among the everlasting ice…
So, judge my horror when I found my stock of magazines
Was chewed into a powder by the mice.

A woeful week went by and not a single pill I had,
Me, that would smoke my forty in a day;
I sighed, I swore, I strode the floor; I thought I would go mad;
The Gospel plugger watched me in dismay.
My brow was wet, my teeth were set, my nerves were rasping raw;
And yet that preacher couldn't understand;
So with despair, I wrestled there—when suddenly I saw
The volume he was holding in his hand.

Then something snapped inside my brain, and with an evil start
The wolf-man in me woke to rabid rage.
"I saved your lousy life", says I, "so show you have a heart,
And tear me out a solitary page".
He shrank and shrivelled at my words; his face went pewter white;
'Twas just as if I'd handed him a blow;
And then—and then he seemed to swell, and grow to Heaven's height,
And in a voice that range, he answered "NO".

I grabbed my loaded rifle and I jabbed it to his chest;
"come on you shrimp, give up that Book", says I.
Well sir, he was a parson, but he stacked up with the best,
And for grit, I got to hand it to the guy.
"If I should let you desecrate this Holy Word", he said,
"My soul would be eternally accursed.
So, go on Bill, I'm ready, you can pump me full of lead
And take it—but you'll have to kill me first".

Now, I'm no foul assassin, though I'm full of sinful ways,
And I knew right there, the fellow had me beat;
For a I felt a yellow mongrel in the glory of his gaze,
And I flung my foolish firearm at his feet.
Then wearily, I turned away, and dropped upon my bunk,

And there I lay and blubbered like a kid.
"Forgive me pard", says I at last, "I've acted like a skunk,
But hid the blasted rifle"—which he did.

And he also hid his Bible, which was maybe just as well,
For the sight of all that paper gave me pain;
And there were crimson moments when I thought I'd go to hell
To have a single cigarette again.
And so I lay, day after day, and brooded dark and deep,
Until one night I thought I'd end it all;
Then rough I roused the preacher, where he stretched pretending sleep,
With his map of horror turned against the wall.

"See here, my pious pal", says I, "I've stood it long enough—
Behold!, I've mixed some strychnine in a cup.
Enough to kill a dozen men—believe me, it's no bluff,
Now watch me, for I'm going to drink it up.
You've seen me bludgeoned with despair, through bitter days and nights,
And now you'll see me squirming as I die.
You're not to blame, you've played the game according to your lights—
But how would Christ have played it?—Well, good bye".

With that I raised the deadly drink and laid it to my lips,
But he was on me with a tiger-bound;
And as we rocked and reeled and locked with wild and wicked grips,
The poison cup went crashing to the ground.
"Don't do it Bill," he madly shrieked, "maybe I acted wrong.
See here's my Bible—use it as you will;
But promise me—you'll read a little as you go along…
You do! Then brother, take it, smoke your fill".

And so I did. I smoked and smoked, from Genesis to Job,
And as I smoked I read each blessed word;
While in the shadow of his bunk I heard him sigh and sob,
And then a most peculiar thing occurred.
I got to reading more and more, and smoking less and less,
'Till just about the time his heart was broke,
Says I, "here take it back, me lad, I've had enough, I guess,
Your paper makes a mighty rotten smoke"!

So then and there, with plea and prayer, he wrestled for my soul,
And I was racked and ravaged by regrets.
But God was good for lo! Next day, there came the police patrol,
With paper for a thousand cigarettes...
So now I'm called "Salvation Bill", I teach the Living Law,
And ballyhoo the Bible with the best;
And if a guy won't listen, why I sock him on the jaw,
And preach the Gospel sitting on his chest.

Robert W. Service 1903 Whitehorse, Yukon Territory

THE BONNIE BANKS O' LOCH LOMOND

By yon bonnie banks, and by yon bonnie braes
Where the sun shines bright on Loch Lomond
There me and my true love spent mony happy days
On the bonnie, bonnie banks o' Loch Lomond.

Chorus
Oh, ye'll tak' the high road, and I'll tak' the low road
And I'll be in Scotland before ye
But trouble it is there, and mony hearts are sair
On the bonnie, bonnie banks o' Loch Lomond.

"Twas there that we parted in yon bonnie glen
On the steep, steep side o' Ben Lomond
Where in purple hue the Highland hills we view
And the moon glints out in the gloamin'.

There the wild flowers spring and the wee birdies sing
And in sunshine the waters are sleepin'
But the broken heart it kens nae second spring again
Though resigned we may be while we're greetin'.

THE GRAMOPHONE AT FOND-DU-LAC

Now Eddie Malone got a swell grammyphone
To draw all the trade to his store;
An' he sez "come along for a season of song,
The like ye've heard nivver before."
Then Dogrib an' Slave an' Yellow Knife brave,
An' Cree in his dinky canoe
Confluated there to see an' to hear
Ed's grammyphone make it's daboo.

Then Ed turned the crank and there on the bank
They squatted like bumps on a log,
For acres around there wasn't a sound,
Not even the howl of a dog.
When out of the horn, there sudden was born
Such a marvelous elegant tone;
An' then like a spell on that audience fell
The voice of it's first grammyphone.

"Bad medicine" cried old tom, The One-eyed
And made for to jump in the lake,
But when no one gave heed to his little stampede,
He guessed he had made a mistake.
Then Roll-In-The-Mud, the Chief of The Blood
Observed in choice Chipawayan,
"You've brought us canned beef, and it's now my belief,
That this here's a case of "canned man"".

Well, though I'm not strong on the Dago in song,
That sure got me goin' for fair

There was Crusoe an' Scotty an' Ma'am Shoeman Hank,
An' Melber an' Bonchy was there.
'Twas silver an' gold, an' sweetness untold,
To hear all those big guinnies sing;
An' thick all around, an' inhalin' the sound,
Them Indians formed in a ring.

So solemn they sat, an' they smoked an' they spat,
But their eyes sort o'glistened an' shone;
Yet nivver a word of aprovin' was heard
'Til that guy Harry Lauder came on.
Then Hunter of Moose, an' his squaw an' papoose
Jest laughed 'till their stomicks was sore;
Six times Eddie set back that record an' yet
They hollered an' hollered for more.

I'll never forget that frame-up you bet;
Them caverns of sunset agleam.
Them still peaks aglow, them shadders below,
An' the lake, like a petrified dream.
The teepees that stood by the edge of the wood;
The evenin' star blinkin' alone;
The peace an' the rest, an' final an' best,
The music of Ed's grammyphone.

Then, sudden an' clear, there rang on my ear
A song mightly simple an' old;
Heart-hungry an' high it thrilled to the sky,
All about "Silver Threads In The Gold."
'Twas tender to tears, an' it brung back the years,
The mem'ries that hallow an' yearn.
'Twas home-love an' joy, 'twas the thought of my boy,
An' right there, I vowed I'd return.

Big Four-fingered Jack, he was right at my back,
An' I saw with a kinda surprise,
That he gazed at the lake with a heart full of ache,
An' the tears irrigated his eyes.
An' sez he "cuss me pard, but that there hits me hard,
I've a Mother, does nuthin' but wait.
She's turned 83, an' she's only got me,
An' I'm scared it'll soon be too late".

On Fond-du-lac's shore I'm hearin' once more
That blessed old grammyphone play.
The summer's all gone, an' I'm still livin' on
In the same old haphazardous way;
Oh I cut out the booze, an' with muscles and thews,
I corralled all the coin to go back,
But it wasn't to be, he'd a Mother, you see,
So I slipped it to Four-fingered Jack.

Robert W. Service (1909)

THE IDEALIST

Oh, You who have daring deeds to tell!
And you who have felt Ambition's spell!
Have you heard of the louse who longed to dwell
In the golden hair of a queen?
He sighed all day and he sighed all night,
And no one could understand it quite,
For the head of a slut is a louse's delight,
But he pined for the head of a queen.

So he left his kinsfolk in merry play,
And off by his lonesome he stole away,
From the home of his youth so bright and gay,
And gloriously unclean.
And at last he came to the palace gate,
And he made his way in a manner straight
(for a louse may go where a man must wait)
To the tiring room of the queen.

The queen she spoke to her tiring maid;
"There's something the matter I am afraid.
To-night ere for sleep my hair ye braid,
Just see what may be seen."
And lo, when they combed that shining hair,
They found him alone in his glory there,
And he cried "I die, but I do not care,
For I've lived in the head of a queen".

Robert W. Service—1905

THE JUNIOR GOD

The junior god looked from his place
In the conning towers of Heaven
And saw the world through a span of space
Like a giant golf ball driven,
And because he was bored (as some gods are)
With high celestial mirth
He took the reins of a shooting star
And steered it down to Earth.

The junior god, 'mid leaf and bud,
Passed on with weary aire
'till lo!, he came to a pool of mud
And some hogs were rolling there.
So in he jumped with gleeful cries
And down he lay supine
For they had no mud in Paradise
And they likewise had no swine!

The junior god forget himself
He squelched mud through his toes
With excited joy of a wonton boy
His reckless laughter rose
'Till tired at last, in a brook nearby,
He washed off every stain
And slowly up to the radiant sky,
He rose, a god again.

The junior god now heads the roll
On the list of heaven's peers
He sits in the house of high control,
And regulates the spheres.
Does he sometimes think, do you suppose,
That even in gods divine
The best, most worthy are not those
Who have wallowed a while with the swine?

Robert W. Service 1903 Whitehorse, Yukon Territory.

THE SQUID-JIGGIN' GROUND

Arthur R. Scammell

Oh...this is the palce where the fishermen gather
With oil-skins and boots and Cape Anns battened down
All sizes of figures with squid lines and jiggers
They congregate here o the squid-jiggin' ground.

Some are workin' their jiggers while others are yarnin'
There's some standin' up and there's more lyin' down
While all kinds of fun, jokes and tricks are begun
As they wait for the squid on the squid-jiggin' ground.

There's men of all ages and boys in the bargain
There's old Billy Cave and there's young Raymond Brown
There's a red rantin' Tory out here in the dory
A-runnin' down squires on the squid-jiggin' ground.

There's men from the harbour and men from the Tickle
In all kinds of motorboats...green, grey and brown
Right yonder is Bobby and with him is Nobby
He's chewin' hard tack on the squid-jiggin' ground.

God bless my sou'wester, there's Skipper John Chaffey
He's the best hand at squid-jiggin' here, I'll be bound
Hello! What's the row? Why, he's jiggin' one now
The very first squid on the squid-jiggin' ground.

The man with the whiskers is old Jacob Steele
He's getting' well up but he's still pretty sound
While Uncle Bob Hawkins wears six pairs of stockin's
Whenever he's out on the squid-jiggin' ground.

Holly smoke! What a scuffle! All hands are excited
'Tis a wonder to me that there's nobody drowned
There's a bustle, confusion, a wonderful hustle
They're all jiggin' squid on the squid-jiggin' ground.

Says Bobby, "The squids are on top of the water,
I just got me jigger 'bout one fathom down"
When a squid in the boat squirted right down his throat
And he's swearin' like mad on the squid-jiggin' ground.

There's poor Uncle Billy, his whiskers are spattered
With spots of the squid juice thats' flyin' around;
One poor little b'y got it right in the eye
But they don't give a damn on the squid-jiggin' ground.

Now if ever you feel inclined to go squiddin'
Leave your white shirts and collars behind in the town
And if you get cranky without yer silk hanky
You'd better steer clear of the squid-jiggin' ground.

THE YARN OF THE 'NANCY BELL'

By W.S. Gilbert

'Twas on the shores that round our coast
From Deal to Ramsgate span,
That I found alone on a piece of stone
An elderly naval man.

His hair was weedy, his beard was long,
And weedy and long was he,
And I heared this wight on the shore recite,
In a singular minor key:

"Oh, I am a cook and a captain bold,
And the mate of the Nancy brig,
And a bo'sun tight, and a midshipmight,
And the crew of the captain's gig."

And he shook his fists and he tore his hair,
Till I really felt afraid
For I couldn't help thinking the man had been drinking,
And so I simply said:

"O, elderly man, it's little I know
Of the duties of men of the sea,
But I'll eat my hand if I understand
How you can possibly be

"At once a cook, and a captain bold,
And the mate of the Nancy brig,
And a bo'sun tight and a midshipmight,
And the crew of the captain's gig."

Then he gave a hitch to his trousers, which
Is a trick all seamen larn,
And having got rid of a thumping quid,
He spun this painful yarn:

"Twas in the good ship Nancy Bell
That we sailed to the Indian sea,
And there on a reef we come to grief,
Which has often occurred to me.

"And pretty nigh all o' the crew was drowned
(There was seventy-seven o' soul),
And only ten of the Nancy's men
Said 'Here!" to the muster-roll.

"There was me and the cook and the captain bold,
And the mate of the Nancy brig
And the bo'sun tight, and a midshipmight,
And the crew of the captain's gig.

"For a month we'd neither vittles nor drink,
Till a-hungry we did feel,
So we drawed a lot, and accordin' shot
The captain for our meal.

"the next lot fell to the Nancy's mate,
And a delicate dish he made;
Then our appetite with the midshipmight,
We seven survivors stayed.

"And then we murdered the bo'sun tight,
And he much resembled pig,
Then we whittled free, did the cook and me,
On the crew of the captain's gig.

"then only the cook and me was left,
And the delicate question, 'Which
Of us two goes to the kettle?" arose
And we argued it out as sich.

"For I loved that cook as a brother, I did,
And the cook he worshipped me;
But we'd both be blowed if we'd either be stowed
In the other chap's hold, you see.

"I'll be eat if you dines off me', says tom,
'Yes, that,' says I, 'you'll be,'—
'I'm boiled if I die, my friend, 'quoth I,
And 'Exactly so,' quoth he.

"Says he, 'Dear James, to murder me
Were a foolish thing to do,
For don't you see that you can't cook me,
While I can—and will—cook you!'

"So he boils the water, and takes the salt
And the pepper in portions true
(Which he never forgot) and some chopped shallot,
And some sage and parsley too.

"Come here,' says he, with a proper pride,
Which his smiling features tell,
"'Twill soothing be if I let you see,
How extremely nice you'll smell.'

"And he stirred it round and round and round,
And he sniffed at the foaming froth;
When I ups with his heels, and smothers his squeals
In the scum of the boiling broth.

"And I eat that cook in a week or less,
And—as I eating be
The last of his chops, why, I almost drops,
For a wessel in sight I see!

"And I never grin, and I never smile,
And I never larf nor play,
But I sit and croak, and a single joke
I have—which is to say:

"Oh, I am a cook and a captain bold,
And the mate of the Nancy brig,
And a bo'sun tight, and a midshipmight,
And the crew of the captain's gig!"

WHERE THE GREAT PEACE RIVER FLOWS

There's a river that is flowing up toward the northern sea
It's not famed in song and story, still it has a charm for me
It has called me from the southland where the starry banner blows
And I've settled down forever where the great Peace River flows.

I've a little moss-chinked cabin just beyond its northern shore
Where I hope to live contented till this span of life is o'er
May life's cares pass lightly o'er me, all its troubles and its woes
Be to me a fleeting memory where the great Peace River flows.

In this little bit of Eden where the sun at midnight gleams
All our girls are just like visions from the pleasant land of dreams
Pretty as our dainty bluebells, fair as our native rose
They make all our lives seem brighter where the great Peace River flows.

We have come from every nation, we have done our very best
To uphold the flag of Britain in this grand and glorious west
And no foeman's feet dare trample on our own true prairie rose
'Tis the emblem of our country where the great Peace River flows.

Where the great Peace River's flowing, where the pretty bluebell grows
And the prairies are a-glowing with the beauty of the rose
Here the sun is always shining, no one sits down here repining
And each cloud has a silver lining where the great Peace River flows.

When I get the final summons from the courthouse in the skies
From the Judge of all the Judges, may He deem it no surprise
If I ask Him just one favour...He may grant it...No one knows
Send me back to fair Alberta where the great Peace River flows.

Breinigsville, PA USA
13 April 2011
259716BV00001B/12/P